EDINBURGH SHOPS
PAST AND PRESENT

Princes Street, looking east from the Mound, *c.* 1928.

PICTORIAL EDINBURGH SERIES

Malcolm Cant

EDINBURGH SHOPS

PAST AND PRESENT

MALCOLM CANT PUBLICATIONS

To
Callum John Gould
my first grandson

First published in 2005 by
Malcolm Cant Publications
13 Greenbank Row
Edinburgh EH10 5SY

Reprinted 2005

ISBN 0 9526099 8 3

British Library Cataloguing-in-Publication Data
A catalogue record for this book is available on request

Book and cover designed by Mark Blackadder

Printed and bound by Bell & Bain Ltd,
Glasgow, Scotland

CONTENTS

BY THE SAME AUTHOR

Marchmont in Edinburgh 1984

Villages of Edinburgh Volume 1 (North) 1986

Villages of Edinburgh Volume 2 (South) 1987

Edinburgh: Sciennes and the Grange 1990

Yerbury: A Photographic Collection 1850–1993 1994

Edinburgh: Gorgie and Dalry 1995

Villages of Edinburgh: An Illustrated Guide Volume 1 (North) 1997

The District of Greenbank in Edinburgh 1998

Villages of Edinburgh: An Illustrated Guide Volume 2 (South) 1999

Old Tollcross, Morningside and Swanston 2001

Marchmont, Sciennes and the Grange 2001

Old Dalry in Edinburgh 2002

Old Gorgie 2002

Edinburgh from the Air: 70 Years of Aerial Photography 2003

Old Dean and Stockbridge 2004

Knowing Your Grandfather 2004

INTRODUCTION AND ACKNOWLEDGEMENTS

The idea for *Edinburgh Shops Past and Present* came from looking again at some of the photographs that I have collected over the years of the typical, family-run corner shop in the days before self-service. Many of the shops sold picture postcards of local street scenes, the most popular of which included the various small businesses. Many of those photographs are still available to collectors but, sadly, the identity of the people involved is quickly being lost. To extend the scope of the book I have included more formal photographs taken of the larger shops, usually in the city centre, which illustrate the way in which such businesses operated before the days of out-of-town shopping malls.

The book has been divided into three parts, between which are two colour sections of various advertisements. Part 1 is devoted to shops selling food and drink, including grocers, wine merchants, fruiterers, dairies, confectioners, butchers, fishmongers, tearooms and bakers. Part 2 is a larger group, of non-food shops, including stationers, tobacconists, newsagents, rag stores, ironmongers, opticians, chemists, shoe shops, furriers, tool shops, jewellers, hairdressers, drapers, cycle shops, book, picture and music shops, public houses, post offices, garden centres and house furnishers. Part 3 includes the department stores which were, and in some cases still are, a feature of Edinburgh's main shopping areas. Included among the older names are J. & R. Allan, the outfitters, in South Bridge and Patrick Thomson's in North Bridge. Of the shops that have survived and are still very much part of the city, there is a good selection of old and new photographs of Frasers, James Gray & Son, Jenners and others.

The colour sections, displaying some fine artwork, include advertisements for specific shops like James Gray & Son (ironmongery), McDowell & Sons (biscuits), R. W. Forsyth (outfitters) and John Donald (china). The individual commodities include Crystalade, the thirst-quenching drink, Cox's gelatine for cooking, Harris & Co.'s Wiltshire bacon, Valetta biscuits and many more.

It is not possible to put together a book of this nature without the assistance of a great number of people. This is particularly the case in locating a sufficient number, and variety, of photographs to make the book worthwhile. The nucleus came from my own collection of Edinburgh photographs built up over many years. This initial selection was greatly enhanced by several pictures lent to me by five collectors of Edinburgh material: A. W. Brotchie; Louise Jenkins; Margeorie Mekie; Pat Scoular; and Robin Sherman. In addition to those collectors, a large group of people allowed me to reproduce material from their family albums. Their names appear below the respective photographs throughout the book.

Other people assisted me with general information and establishing the locations of some of the pictures. In alphabetical order they are: Mrs J. Aikman; Miss L. P. Aikman; Kevin Aitchison; Ian Barry; Andrew Broom; Ronald M. Calder; Kate and Robin Cavaye; Colin Dale; Douglas Glass; Kenny Gunn-Russell; Joyce Horberry; May Hoy; Mrs Hutchison; Martin Johnson; Annie Kaylor; Rena Lister; Lindsay Lorimer; Tom Martin; Hamish Mearns; Fred Murray; Mrs Betty Russell; Norman Scott; Mrs Sheila Scott; Brian Seftor; Kenneth Sinclair; Bill Smith; David Speed; Walter Telfer; and Mr & Mrs Wheelan. I was also given a lot of assistance on photographic matters from Ian Goddard, Douglas Hunter and Peter Stubbs. My thanks also go to the managers and staff of Scotmid Co-operative Society Ltd, James Gray & Son, Jenners, House of Fraser and Hamilton & Inches.

Edinburgh is very well served by numerous libraries and archives which I have relied on for research, particularly the Edinburgh Room of the Central Library. Others, whose staff have been very helpful, are: the Corstorphine Trust; Edinburgh City Archives; National Archives of Scotland; and Scotsman Publications Ltd. In the Gorgie and Dalry areas I was assisted by the *Gorgie Dalry Gazette* and the Heart of Midlothian Football Club.

After I had finished writing the book the serious business of publication began: Nicola Wood edited the script to her usual high standard; Mark Blackadder brought the basic material to life with his page and cover design; Oula Jones made everything accessible with a comprehensive index; and Neville Moir supervised all aspects of production. Without the commitment of those professional people I would not be able to publish my own books.

As always, I thank my wife Phyllis and the members of our ever-increasing extended family for their interest and assistance with numerous tasks.

Malcolm Cant
2005

PART 1: FOOD SHOPS ❧

Part 1 has approximately sixty-five pictures showing the many shops involved in the supply of food and drink to the population of Edinburgh. The photographs have been arranged, primarily, by trade, starting with the grocers which are the largest group. Some shops, like Liptons, Lows and St Cuthbert's Co-operative Association Ltd (now Scotmid) were almost household names, whereas others were much smaller, family-run businesses serving a particular locality. It has obviously not been possible to include anything like all Edinburgh shops, but those which have been included are very representative of the city in general: Henderson the wine merchant at Gorgie Square; Kemp the grocer at Restalrig; McGregor the provision merchant at Marchmont; Carnie the grocer in Leith; and Horberry, the grocer and post office at Warrender Park.

The next group of shops is the dairies, many of them established at a time when milk was distributed in pitchers, stacked on horse-drawn carts or small hand-carts. The hand-carts included two- three- and four-wheeled models, some of which, when fully laden, must have been quite heavy for the delivery boys.

Butchers and fishmongers are also well represented, many of the proprietors and staff appearing in the photographs, usually taken outside the shop where the light would have

❧ CRANSTONHILL BAKERY
Cranstonhill Bakery was established at No. 6 Jeffrey Street in 1902 and moved to No. 299 Canongate (seen here) about ten years later, where it remained until 1951. *Courtesy of Robin Sherman.*

been better. Of particular interest are: Whiteford's staff herding turkeys in Main Street, Davidson's Mains; a large staff at Campbell's in Dalry Road and also at Anderson's in Castle Street; McPherson's, the fishmonger, in Gorgie Road; and a fish and chip shop advertising fish suppers at 2d in 1909.

Some of the bakers had part of their premises given over to a tearoom where they sold their own products, notably Torrance in Morningside which was famous for its Kettledrum Shortbread. Two very similar photographs have been included in the Tollcross area: one, in Earl Grey Street, of Nairns, the large bakery chain; and the other, a small family business run by Andrew Hamilton in Bread Street. Tearooms were, and still are, very numerous, some of them quite innovative in their attempts to attract particular custom, such as: the Neuk at Corstorphine, a favourite rendezvous point for the local cycling club; the Refreshment Rooms for golfers on the Braid Hills; Shearers, which served breakfasts on Portobello Promenade; and, most exclusive of all, the Edinburgh Cafe Company and Kardomah Cafe on Princes Street. The last page of Part 1 includes two photographs which do not easily fit into any particular category. The first is Hutton's shop in Juniper Green, which had fruit and vegetables in one half and china and fancy goods in the other. For human

❧ TODD'S, FRUITERER AND ART FLORIST
The photograph shows the staff of Todd's outside the shop at No. 31 Shandwick Place some time prior to 1921 when the shop fronts were greatly altered. After 1921 Todd's moved to No. 2 Hope Street.
Courtesy of Margeorie Mekie.

interest, however, there is little to equal the second photograph, Mrs Murray's General Store – 'Mangling Done Here, By Electricity'.

Where known, the dates of the photographs and the identity of the people have been given but, unfortunately, many are unknown. This is true of the two photographs that appear in this short introduction. Cranstonhill Bakery, on the corner of Jeffrey Street and Canongate was famous for 'Marriage, Birthday and Ornamental Cakes' as well as being 'Purveyors for Picnic and Social Parties'. The other picture is of the staff outside Todd's of Shandwick Place, Fruiterer and Art Florist.

A few advertisements and window displays have also been included in Part 1 showing some of the commodities for sale in the respective shops. These include: the window display for Oxydol and Dreft by William Low & Co; Lux, Shredded Wheat and Diploma by John Horberry; and fresh strawberries every morning from Kelly's of Morningside Road.

Some of the shops depicted were in business for only a short time, whilst others remained in the same family for many years. Others, like Low's, the grocers, were absorbed into larger food chains, and some, like St Cuthbert's Co-operative Association, took on a completely new identity in the form of Scotmid Co-operative Society Ltd.

LIPTON, PROVISION MERCHANTS

In Edinburgh in the early 1900s, Lipton's had shops at North Bridge, Shandwick Place, Earl Grey Street and Kirkgate. The photograph shows the premises at No. 25 Shandwick Place at an unknown date. The right-hand window is entirely devoted to tea which was one of Lipton's main commodities, advertised under the slogan 'Drink and Enjoy Lipton's Tea: Largest Sale in the World'. Lipton's Special is priced at 1/2d (6p) per pound, backed up by all that the housewife needs to know about the competition: 'Better than sold by any other firm at 1/4d'. The left-hand window is filled with Finest Quality Smoked Rolled Bacon and Finest Quality Pale Bacon, much of which appears to be displayed in the open air. What looks like a bacon slicer is sitting at the door to the left of the assistant with the striped apron. *Malcolm Cant Collection.*

R. & T. GIBSON LTD, PROVISION MERCHANTS

R. & T. Gibson was founded in 1848 at No. 98 Princes Street but within a decade had moved a few doors along to larger premises at No. 93. In 1889 the shop was extended to include No. 5 Frederick Street. Advertising material from around 1890 describes the business as 'a veritable trade palace ... a superb establishment in a superb thoroughfare ... fitted with two waiting rooms, one for the ladies and one for the gentlemen ... and stabling used by the firm in delivery of goods'. The Balmoral Restaurant and Cafe, located on the upper floors, was part of the business.

   In 1950 the shop and restaurant were acquired by a group of Edinburgh businessmen, headed by Lord Provost Sir Andrew Murray, who subsequently sold the property (but not the actual business) to Littlewoods. This undated photograph shows the interior of the Princes Street shop at the height of the Gibsons' success as 'Tea and Coffee Salesmen, Grocers and Italian Warehousemen'. They were the first in Scotland to stock Harris's Wiltshire bacon. *Courtesy of Hamish Mearns.*

JOHN HENDERSON, PROVISION MERCHANTS

This unusually-shaped building occupied by John Henderson, the provision merchants, stood in what was called Gorgie Square or 'the Auld Square' near Alexander Drive, off Gorgie Road. The shop, appropriately called 'the Auld Hoose', and the much older building on the left of the picture, were demolished in the early 1930s for the construction of the Poole's Roxy Cinema. The picture, taken around 1930, shows the proprietor, Tom Henderson, outside the shop, which was founded by his father, John Henderson, in the early 1900s. As befits the location, the outside of the shop is festooned with many advertisements. From left to right, those which can be read include: Fry's Chocolate, Estd. 1728, Patronize the Oldest Firm in the Trade; Bovril; Hudson's Soap, For the People; Rowntrees Cocoa; Lyon's Tea; Sandeman Ports; Crawford's York Biscuits; Bourneville, the Last Word in Cocoa; Colman's Starch; and Van Houten's Cocoa, Best and Goes Farthest.
Courtesy of Rena Lister, née Dunn.

EXTERIOR OF SAUGHTON WINE STORES

After Henderson's premises in Gorgie Square were demolished in the early 1930s, Tom Henderson had new premises built in 1932 with the assistance of Paterson, the joiner, slightly further out of town, at No. 536 Gorgie Road. The site was chosen in anticipation of custom coming from the new houses being built at Stenhouse, and farmers attending the Gorgie Cattle Market nearby. The photograph shows the owner of the shop in the doorway, with his son-in-law, David Dunn, on the right, and William Keppie, an assistant, on the left. The left-hand window has adverts for Symington's Coffee Essence, Made in a Moment, and Hartley's Blackcurrant Jam. The right-hand window has a wide variety of wines and spirits, particularly Australian Sweet Wines and Digger Brand Australian Burgundy. The gate on the left of the shop led to a small yard with a garage and storage shed, to which wholesalers made deliveries. One of the two delivery bikes, used by message-boys to deliver orders, is on the right of the picture. *Courtesy of Rena Lister, née Dunn.*

❧ Interior of Saughton Wine Stores

Inside the Saughton Wine Stores, *c.* 1932, with David Dunn on the left and his assistant, William Keppie, on the right, surrounded by neatly stacked shelves and a host of well-known brand names of the day: Lyon's Puff Pastry; Chivers' Jellies; Hendry's Still Drinks; Brazil Oranges; McVitie & Price's Biscuits, and many more. *Courtesy of Rena Lister, née Dunn.*

❧ G. L. Miller's Fruit Store

In the 1930s, G. L. Miller's Fruit Store was located in a timber-built shop in Bridge Road, Colinton, on a site later developed by Harwell's of Colinton and then W. H. Smith. The left-hand window is devoted to fresh fruit with display signs, 'Delicious' and 'Eating', and the right-hand window is filled with confectionery.

❧ Anderson, the Greengrocer

The exact position of this 'Quaint Bit of Morrison Street' is not known but it was on the north side of the road, somewhere east of the present Edinburgh International Conference Centre. Up until about 1887 that part of Morrison Street was called Castle Barns. Although the photograph describes the location as 'quaint', many of the surrounding tenements were in a very poor state of repair. *Malcolm Cant Collection.*

McKechnie's Fruiterer and Florist

In 1926, A. F. McKechnie, the proprietor of McKechnie's Fruiterer and Florist, lived at No. 8 The Crescent, Gorgie, which lay between Westfield Road and Alexander Drive. The shop was on the south side of Gorgie Road, a few doors west of the junction with Robertson Avenue. The main advertisement is for Fry's Chocolate but the top of the window has a display panel for 'Wreaths, Crosses, Bouquets, Sprays, Ect. [*sic*] Made to Order: Charges Moderate'. The upper part of the window also has the reverse image of the words 'MacGregor, Milliner' apparently painted onto the glass. It is, in fact, the reflection of the shop front on the other side of the road at No. 298 Gorgie Road. *Malcolm Cant Collection.*

Three Dalry Grocers

On 11 September 1909, 'J.B. c/o Mrs Robb No. 143 Dalry Road' wrote to Mr Jackson, the grocer, High Street, Crail saying that 'this is a photo of two of the chaps beside me in my new job' but unfortunately the identity of the shop proprietor and its location were not disclosed. Presumably it was one of the many small grocers' shops in the area at the beginning of the twentieth century. *Malcolm Cant Collection.*

George Donaldson & Sons

George Donaldson & Sons, Grocers and Wine Merchants, was established in 1829 and went on to open shops at No. 26 West Maitland Street and Nos. 59 & 61 Newington Road. The undated photograph, taken in Canning Street Lane, shows one of the firm's drivers with the well-groomed horse and light cart for deliveries. In 1892 Donaldson's advertised themselves as: 'Dealers in Home, Foreign & Colonial Produce. Families in Town and Country supplied with GROCERIES, WINES and MALT LIQUORS of the Choicest Qualities, at the Lowest Cash Prices. Agents for Kinloch's Catalan and other Wines'. *Courtesy of Mrs Elsie Burnie.*

❧ Wm. Low & Co., Home Street

William Low & Co. was at No. 48 Home Street from 1897, adjacent to the Commercial Bank of Scotland, at No. 46. Part of the Bank's window sign can be seen on the right of the picture. If the single letter 'R', on the left, is part of the name Lachlan Sinclair, bakers and confectioners, then the photograph was probably taken in the early 1900s. Most of the male members of staff are almost regimental in style, with fresh aprons, rolled shirt sleeves, waistcoats and stiff collars. Both windows are crammed with advertisements, particularly various blends of tea, including Ceylon at 1/6d per pound and Willow Blend at 1/4d. The left-hand window has a wide range of hams and bacons, all individually priced. *Courtesy of W. Telfer.*

❧ Wm Low & Co., Dalry Road

Wm. Low & Co. also had a branch at No. 58 Dalry Road, photographed here *c.* 1950, with the manager and two female assistants. The well-stocked shelves contain a wide variety of products: Kellogg's All-Bran and Rice Krispies; Crosse & Blackwell's Soups; Atora beef suet; and Spry cooking fat. In the right-hand corner, the open box on the floor contains Fyffe's bananas packed in straw. *Courtesy of W. Telfer.*

Courtesy of Joyce Horberry.

Courtesy of Joyce Horberry.

WM. LOW & CO., DALRY ROAD DISPLAY

The Dalry Road branch of Wm. Low & Co. entered for the Thomas Hedley's display competition for Oxydol and Dreft in the 1950s. The advertising slogans are: 'For Brighter Washdays Use Oxydol for Whites and Colours' and 'The Modern Woman Uses Dreft for Silks and Woollens'. *Courtesy of W. Telfer.*

WM. LOW & CO. LTD, MORNINGSIDE ROAD

Wm. Low & Co. Ltd, Grocers & Provision Merchants, of No. 320 Morningside Road, had the advantage of a smart delivery van. The vehicle is a Commer 6/8 cwt. light van £150 ex works, supplied by the Edinburgh dealer, James Ross of Lochrin, *c.* 1933. Prior to the introduction of delivery vans, young men would enter the grocery business as delivery boys using message bikes, and be paid at the rate of 15/- (75p) per week, plus tips. On promotion to junior member of the shop staff, their weekly wages were increased to 18/- from which they were required to buy, from Hewat's, the overall specialists, their own uniforms of white shirts, jackets and aprons, and to pay for their weekly laundry bill. *Malcolm Cant Collection.*

❧ St Cuthbert's, Gorgie Road

Right. This very small shop, with a fairly large staff, remains something of an enigma as the exact location is uncertain. There is a suggestion of the number '10' quite low down on the face of the building, to the left of the group. The photograph could be No. 10 Gorgie Road where St Cuthbert's opened its Tynecastle Grocery branch on 18 March 1882. It was replaced by a much larger store in 1889 to include 'fleshing, drapery and boots'. *Malcolm Cant Collection.*

❧ St Cuthbert's, Juniper Green

Below right. The staff and delivery van driver of Juniper Green Co-operative Society Ltd. with their very latest acquisition. The Juniper Green Co-operative was absorbed by St Cuthbert's Co-operative Association Ltd in 1915. The branch at No. 589 Lanark Road closed on 17 April 1982 much to the disappointment of local people. *Malcolm Cant Collection.*

❧ St Cuthbert's First Shop

Below. St Cuthbert's Co-operative Association Ltd. opened its first retail shop at No. 50 Fountainbridge on 4 November 1859 when the paid up capital of the company was a little over £30. *From* First Fifty Years of St Cuthbert's Co-operative Association Ltd, 1859-1909.

❧ ST CUTHBERT'S, PIERSHILL PLACE

Above. A staff of twenty-one (nine men and twelve women) outside the shop at No. 9 Piershill Place sometime between 1919 and 1926. Henry Cumming Lawrence is fifth from the right. The branch was opened on 30 November 1901. *Courtesy of Alex Lawrence (son of Henry Cumming Lawrence).*

❧ ST CUTHBERT'S, CORSTORPHINE HIGH STREET

Left. The staff of St Cuthbert's Co-operative Association Ltd., *c.* 1920, outside the premises in Corstorphine High Street. The tall gentleman in the centre of the front row is Jim Munro, with Jean Robson (his future wife) on his left. The premises were opened in 1905, although St Cuthbert's had been in Corstorphine in smaller premises since 1902. *Courtesy of Mrs Mae Watson, née Munro (daughter of Jim and Jean Munro).*

❧ R. Bowie, Provision Merchant

R. Bowie, the provision merchant, occupied a typical grocer's corner shop at the junction of Watson Crescent and Ritchie Place from at least 1900. The photograph is dated *c*. 1912. He lived nearby at No. 91 Harrison Road with his wife and family. On the right of the photograph, the much smaller shop is run by B. Rough as a news agent, tobacconist, grocer and confectioner. *Malcolm Cant Collection.*

❧ Kemp's Corner

Charles Arthur Kemp Snr came to Edinburgh from Orkney in 1906, and in 1908 he bought the premises on the corner of Restalrig Road South and Marionville Road. His first day's takings, on 21 December 1908, amounted to 16/- (80p). Helped by his intimate knowledge of the Orkney markets for butter, eggs, cheese and rabbits, he built up a very active trade, both in the retail shop and as a wholesaler of Orkney products in Edinburgh. The shop also stocked a wide variety of wines and spirits including: Southalia White Wine, Produce of Australia; Pluto Fine Golden South African Sherry, Empire Produce; and Fine Old Tawny Port. There was also Kemp's own blended Finest Old Scotch Whisky, Barclay Perkins Imperial Stout, and Bass, bottled and corked on the premises. In 1934, Charles Arthur Kemp Jnr joined his father in the business after a short apprenticeship with J. & J. Tod of Edinburgh, and maintained the family business until 1982 when he retired. The photograph, *c*. 1935, shows, from left to right: Alex Davidson, Nancy Dippie, Robert Harris, Charles Arthur Kemp Snr, and Catherine Kemp. *Courtesy of Charles Arthur Kemp Jnr.*

❧ Kemp's Pavement Stone

For many years the shop location was always known as 'Kemp's Corner', which has now been commemorated by the City in a stone plaque in the pavement outside the shop. *Photograph by Phyllis M. Cant.*

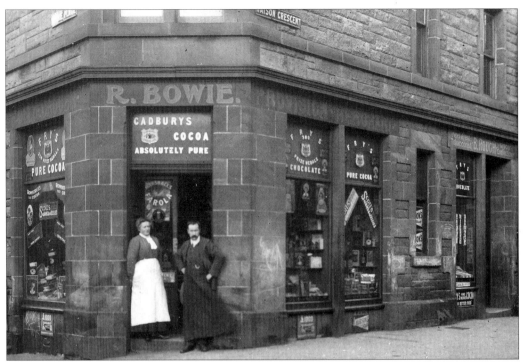

W. D. McGregor, Provision Merchant

W. D. McGregor, Provision Merchant, at No. 21d Strathearn Road in the 1950s. The shop was opened in 1905 by William Davidson McGregor who came to Edinburgh from Caithness, and is still in the hands of the McGregor family. *Courtesy of Ken McGregor.*

John Carnie, Grocer & Spirit Merchant

The fully-laden delivery cart, with the delivery man and the grocer posing nonchalantly for the camera, is outside John Carnie's shop at No. 13 Couper Street, Leith. Mr Carnie took over the business of grocer and spirit merchant from William Adamson in 1904 and ran the business until 1923 when it was bought by John Dalgleish. The sign, protruding from the front of the adjacent property says 'Houses to Let' by Boak & Calder, House Factors & Insurance Agents, No. 137 Great Junction Street. *Courtesy of Robin Sherman.*

Blanche & Christison, Wine Merchants

The name Blanche, in Edinburgh, was synonymous with the businesses of grocers and wine merchants. Blanche & Christison, Wine & Italian Warehousemen, occupied extensive premises on the corner of Slateford Road and Shandon Place from 1898. The partnership existed until around 1916 after which the Slateford Road shop was run by John W. Blanche (in addition to shops at Dalry, Corstorphine and in the city centre) until 1963. The photograph, dated 1906, shows the Slateford Road premises with a selection of whiskies for sale at 2/6d and 3/- (15p) per bottle. *Courtesy of Margeorie Mekie.*

HORBERRY, PROVISION MERCHANT

Right. John James Horberry, born in 1875, opened his first shop at the corner of Warrender Park Road and Spottiswoode Street in 1901. His son, William Anderson Horberry, joined the firm in 1920 and remained there all his working life apart from the duration of the Second World War. The third generation, Eric William Horberry, served his apprenticeship with Dymock Howden, the famous Wine Merchants & Italian Warehousemen, of George Street, before joining his father in 1957. After thirty years in the business, Eric Horberry closed the shop in 1987, ending an unbroken period of eighty-seven years in the same family. During that time the Horberry family built up a substantial customer base, both as a family grocer and, in the earlier years, as the local post office. The photograph shows John James Horberry and his staff outside the shop at No. 77 Warrender Park Road. *Courtesy of Mrs Joyce Horberry.*

HORBERRY, PROVISION MERCHANT

Below right. When Marchmont was built in the 1880s, the plan included several shop units usually located at the street intersections. The units were quickly occupied by traders eager to establish themselves in the new district where many of them also lived. From left to right the shops are: Spottiswoode Dairy run by K. Greig; Horberry, Provision Merchant and Post Office, run by John J. Horberry who lived at No. 6 Arden Street; Fruiterer & Confectioner (No. 73) run by Miss Margaret Reid who lived at No. 20 Marchmont Road; and the Chemist & Druggist (at No. 71 with the mortar and pestle above the door) run by William Gibb who lived at No. 2 Arden Street. The photograph is believed to date from the early 1920s. *Courtesy of Mrs Joyce Horberry.*

HORBERRY'S SPECIALITIES

Far right. John J. Horberry circulated advertising leaflets from time to time drawing the public's attention to his wide range of products both in the grocery department and the post office: New Season's Marmalade, made on the premises 8¼d per lb., jar returned; the Warrender Writing Pad 200 pages 1/- each; and local view postcards 1¼d each. *Courtesy of Mrs Joyce Horberry.*

PENS, INK, PENCILS, Etc. Etc.

Note Only Address—
JOHN HORBERRY,
77 Warrender Park Road.

Introducing A FEW *Specialities*

THE SHOP FOR QUALITY

Warrender Park Post Office,
77 Warrender Park Road, Edinburgh.

AGENT FOR
ANDREW MELROSE & CO'S
FAMED TEAS.

DUNBAR'S AERATED WATERS.

Parkinson's, Doncaster, Butter Scotch
Etc. Etc.

"THE SHOP FOR QUALITY" WARRENDER PARK ROAD, EDINBURGH.

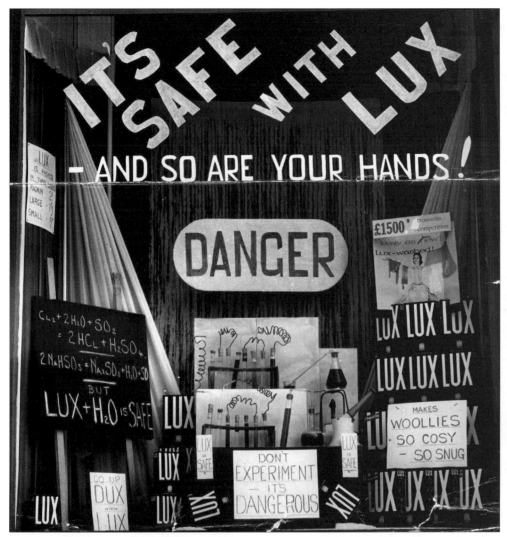

❧ Horberry Window Display for Lux

The basis of the advertisement is LUX+H_2O is SAFE but it is preceded by two less pleasant chemical formulae. The upper one: $Cl_2 + 2H_2O + SO_2 = 2HCl + H_2SO_4$ translates as chlorine with water and sulphur dioxide gives hydrochloric acid and sulphuric acid. The second formula does not balance chemically and should end SO_2 instead of SO. This translates as sodium bisulphite which, on heating, gives sodium sulphite, plus water, plus sulphur dioxide. Wash day should really be simpler to understand. *Courtesy of Mrs Joyce Horberry.*

❧ Horberry Window Display for Shredded Wheat

The Shredded Wheat advertisement is represented by a boxing ring in the centre of the window in which one contestant (who presumably had Shredded Wheat for his breakfast) has just floored his weaker opponent. The window was dressed for the *Daily Express* National Shop Window Display Contest. *Courtesy of Mrs Joyce Horberry.*

❧ Horberry Window Display for Diploma

This Horberry window, advertising Diploma, the English Crustless Cheese, is also dressed for the *Daily Express* National Shop Window Display Contest. The potential customer is told that Diploma Cheese and Biscuits are 'appetising', but what is perhaps more difficult to swallow is their further assertion that they are also 'An Aid to Digestion'. The lady on the phone (to the right of the vase) is, however, determined to order her favourite cheese, as she repeats, 'No, it must be Diploma'. *Courtesy of Mrs Joyce Horberry.*

❧ Cumnock's Creamery

Above. The staff and delivery man of the Cumnock Creamery Co. Ltd outside the premises at No. 159 Morrison Street, *c.* 1920.

❧ James Morren, the Dairyman

Top right. Dairyman James Morren delivered milk daily in the Dalry area.

❧ Greenend Dairy

Middle right. Greenend Dairy, run by Thomas Wood, was probably located on the east side of Gilmerton Road near to Liberton Golf Course.

❧ Dalry Dairy

Right. Dalry Dairy, run by M. Allan, was at No. 22 Dalry Road beside Frank Kumerer, the Pork Butcher. *All Malcolm Cant Collection.*

Craiglea Dairy

Left. Craiglea Dairy, at No. 98 Comiston Road, was run by Mr Peter McKay and his wife Mrs Jane McKay, née Muirhead, from 1930 to 1937. Milk was supplied early each morning by William Wilkie of Comiston Farm and then poured into bottles or cans. The photograph shows Mrs Jane McKay, on the right, and her assistant in the shop, *c.* 1934. Among the items for sale are many well-known brands of the day: McVitie & Price's Cheddar Assortment; Carr's Biscuits; Crawford's Rover Assorted; Macfarlane Lang's Gypsy Creams; and Lyon's Chocolate Cream Bars. The bracket for the original gas lighting can be seen to the right of the door.
Courtesy of Mrs Marion C. Wright, née McKay.

Carruthers Dairy

The photograph shows, *c.*1910, Thomas Carruthers' dairy at No. 5 Gillespie Place, opposite the Barclay Church. In 1874 the previous proprietor, Thomas Nisbet, sold the dairy to Thomas Carruthers whose name remained on the fascia until 1950. After 1950, the dairy was run by Mrs M. J. Boothroyd who lived at No. 9 Marchmont Street and was probably Mr Carruthers' daughter. Mr Carruthers always lived within walking distance of the shop, firstly at No. 32 Wright's Houses, then at No. 42 Bruntsfield Place and latterly at No. 9 Marchmont Street. His eldest son, also Thomas, was a golf club maker at the Golfer's Tryst, Braid Hills. The photograph shows what looks like a family group, probably with Mr Carruthers on the right.
Courtesy of Margeorie Mekie.

Comiston Road Dairy

Comiston Road Dairy, or Aitken's Dairy, photographed *c.* 1918, at No. 99 Comiston Road. The proprietor, Mrs Aitken, who lived at No. 38 Braid Crescent, is in the centre, Nell Hannah is on the right, but the identity of the young girl on the left has not been established. The light barrow parked on the pavement was one of several used to deliver milk and cream to neighbouring houses. Deliveries were made first thing in the morning and also at intervals during the day. The family of Nell Hannah still recalls being told of Nell's most important customer around 1910: a half-penny worth of cream to be taken to 'the big house' Hermitage of Braid.
Courtesy of Mrs June Clark, née Filler.

CHRISTMAS TURKEYS AT DAVIDSON'S MAINS.

❧ BARTIE, BUTCHER

Above. George Bartie, the butcher, operated from very modest premises at the south-west end of Inglis Green Road in the 1920s and 1930s. He is seen here, preparing for the next cut, on his delivery rounds outside the Longstone Inn, which, at that time, was owned by the Murray family.
Malcolm Cant Collection.

❧ WHITEFORD'S TURKEYS

Top right. Turkeys galore being herded for Whiteford, the butcher, in Main Street, Davidson's Mains, *c.* 1934. The man second from the left is David Whiteford, master butcher, whose shop was on the south side of Main Street. *Courtesy of Robin Sherman.*

❧ WHITEFORD'S TURKEYS

Right. The turkeys turn off Main Street into The Green, with Whiteford's shop in the background.
Courtesy of Mrs M. M. Morton.

18

❧ CAMPBELL, BUTCHER

Left. J. B. Campbell, the family butcher, was at Nos. 69 & 71 Dalry Road. The photograph, taken in the early 1950s, shows, from left to right: John Campbell; Lottie Campbell; Charlie Neilson; Margaret Campbell; Duncan (surname unknown); Addison Campbell; James B. Campbell and a cat.
Courtesy of Mr and Mrs J. D. Hadden.

❧ CUTHILL, BUTCHER

Below left. The original shop frontage of Cuthill, Butcher and Poulterer, established in 1892 in Warrender Park Road. The photograph was taken in 1983.
Malcolm Cant Collection.

❧ JOHN ANDERSON & SONS, FISHMONGERS, POULTERERS, ICE MERCHANTS AND GAME DEALERS

Below. A large staff, suitably dressed for the occasion, outside the premises at No. 29 Castle Street. The window has signs for 'Tay Salmon' and 'Fish for Easter'.
Malcolm Cant Collection.

❧ Fish Restaurant

The location of this fish restaurant, offering fish suppers at 2d, is almost certainly No. 138 Gorgie Road. The man second from the right is John Cormack. The poster on the window says: 'Tis true Pringle's pictures are the best'; and there are several football-related photographs in the window. The door sign appears to say: 'Give Neil's Suppers a Trial'. The photograph comes from a picture postcard, signed by 'Willie', posted in Edinburgh on 1 February 1909, and addressed to G. Key c/o Chelsea F. C., Stamford Bridge, Near London. George Key and Willie Porteous both appear in one of the photographs in the window when they played for Hearts the year they won the Scottish Cup in 1901. *Courtesy of Robin Sherman.*

❧ Liston & Brown, Fishmongers

Mr Liston and Mr Brown took over the fishmonger's business at No. 67 Slateford Road from Robert Langlands in 1917, and remained there until 1939. After 1939 the business was run by Mrs M. Brown until she retired in 1955. The delivery van appears to be the same model as that used by Wm. Low & Co. Ltd, of Morningside Road (see page 9), namely, a Commer 6/8 cwt. van £150 ex works, supplied by the Edinburgh dealer, James Ross of Lochrin. *Malcolm Cant Collection.*

❧ McPherson's, Fishmongers

McPherson's, the fishmongers, was started *c.* 1905 by Annie McPherson, née Sutherland, who came to Edinburgh from a fishing family in Golspie, Sutherland. The first shop, at No. 98 Gorgie Road, had a small staircase at the back which led to the family home on the first floor of the tenement at No. 96. The business, which still operates from No. 102 Gorgie Road, has now been run by four generations of the same family: the founder from 1905; Donald Sutherland McPherson from 1920; Donald Alexander McPherson from 1951; and Steven McPherson from 1983. The photograph shows McPherson's cart outside No. 102 Gorgie Road ready to take part in one of the Infirmary Pageants in the 1920s.
Courtesy of the McPherson family.

TORRANCE, BAKER

The bakery, confectionery business and tea room were run by the Torrance family at No. 2 Comiston Road from *c.* 1894. They also manufactured and distributed the famous Kettledrum Shortbread. There was a staircase at ground-floor level which led to the tea room at first-floor level, from which patrons were able to watch the passing scene whilst sampling items from the menu. The delivery boys (with their baskets lying on the pavement) can be seen to the left of the corner entrance. William Torrance, the founder of the firm, was one of three Morningside Town Councillors who gifted the station clock to the citizens of Edinburgh in 1910. *Malcolm Cant Collection.*

NAIRN BROS. LTD, BAKER

Below left. The photograph shows two assistants outside Nairn's, the bakers, at No. 11 Earl Grey Street in 1937. The window has been specially dressed to celebrate the coronation of King George VI and Queen Elizabeth in 1937. Nairn's opened the Earl Grey Street branch in 1933 by which time it already had about sixteen branches in Edinburgh, controlled from the head office in Iona Street. The business was established in 1860 by William Nairn, described at that time as a pastry baker, at No. 18 Riddle's Court in Leith. *Courtesy of Mrs F. Christie, née Telfer.*

A. HAMILTON, BAKER & CONFECTIONER

Left. Andrew Hamilton, Baker & Confectioner, was at No. 49 Bread Street for a few years only in the early 1920s. The photograph, taken *c.* 1923, shows his fiancée, Lily McKenzie, on the right and one of the shop assistants on the left. In the late 1930s, Andrew Hamilton was a partner in the bakery business, Thompson & Hamilton, firstly at Bonaly Road (now Harrison Gardens) and later at Colinton Road, near Happy Valley.
Courtesy of Mrs Sheila Hutchison, née Hamilton.

THE NEUK

The photograph shows The Neuk, Confectioner, Tobacconist and Post Office at No. 267 Corstorphine Road in 1952 when the business was run by Mrs Janie Lockie with the assistance of her husband, Andrew. They both appear in the picture: Andrew Lockie is the gentleman standing at the kerb and Janie Lockie is immediately to his right, walking to the left of the picture. Mrs Lockie was the postmistress at The Neuk well into her eighties and died at Corstorphine Hospital at the age of 102. Andrew Lockie, an engineer, was the son of Katharine F. Lockie, the author of *Picturesque Edinburgh* published in 1899. The small boy, who can just be seen at the gate on the right, is David Williamson. Although the business was owned by the Lockie family when the photograph was taken, the name of the previous proprietor, Miss E. C. Frier, is still showing below the name, The Neuk.
Courtesy of Ian Williamson.

THE NEUK

This much earlier, undated picture, shows the original Neuk Tea Rooms on Corstorphine Road, advertising Luncheons, Ices and Confectionery, with the owners, the Misses Frier, at the doorway. In the 1920s and 1930s, The Neuk was the rendezvous point on Sunday mornings for the Corstorphine Cycling Club.
Courtesy of Ian Williamson.

REFRESHMENT ROOMS

This photograph comes from a picture postcard dated 1924. Presumably the Refreshment Rooms, East End, Braid Hills were situated on or near Braid Hills Road and would have been popular with golfers and walkers. Unfortunately no other details of the exact location or the proprietor have been traced.
Courtesy of A. W. Brotchie.

SHEARER'S RESTAURANT

Left. Shearer's Restaurant and Tea Rooms did a roaring trade on the Promenade in Portobello's hey-day at the beginning of the twentieth century. Its advertisement on the side of the building says: 'Refreshments, Breakfasts and Teas, Aerated Waters 1d and 1½d, Dinners 1/- & 1/3, Cigars and Cigarettes'. Below the flag, on the left of the picture, there is another restaurant, Sea Garden Cafe, and there are apartments to let in the tenement above. *Courtesy of Robin Sherman.*

THE EDINBURGH CAFE CO.

Below left and far left. The Oak Hall, with its panelled walls, pillars and ornate archways, was a very popular eating place in 1911 when this photograph was taken. The Edinburgh Cafe Co., Confectioners and Restaurateurs, was established in 1881 at No. 88 Princes Street where it remained until 1886. The business then moved to much grander premises at No. 70 under its new manager, A. E. Phillips. For many years the business was confined to confectioner and restaurateur, but in 1922 a fruit and flower stall was added, and a tobacco kiosk the following year. Whether this was a sign of a failing business is not known, but in 1924 The Edinburgh Cafe Co. closed. The premises were then taken over by D. S. Crawford Ltd, Bakers & Confectioners, whose Bellevue bakery supplied several Crawford's shops throughout Edinburgh. The smaller picture on the left shows the exterior of the building at No. 70 Princes Street. On the extreme right, a small section can be seen of the adjacent building, occupied by the North British & Mercantile Insurance Company. *Courtesy of Robin Sherman.*

KARDOMAH CAFE

Left. The delights of the Kardomah Cafe at No. 111 Princes Street might never have been known had it not been for the diligence of one of its patrons who wrote to her friend, Mrs Jackson at No. 12 Carlton Terrace, Edinburgh on 10 May 1906: 'The popularity of the Kardomah Coffee is quite phenomenal. It is roasted for each day's requirements and ground for each purchaser and may be sampled in the Kardomah Cafe (4d per cup with cream & biscuits)'. *Malcolm Cant Collection.*

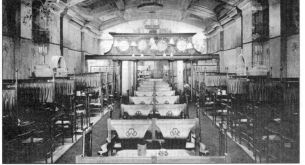

J. Hutton, Confectioner

Standing outside Hutton's shop at No. 558 Lanark Road, Juniper Green are, from left to right: Mrs I. Hutton; Mrs M. Hutton; and Mrs M. Ireland. The left-hand window has fruit and confections, and the right-hand window is given over to china and fancy goods. The sign above the door says: 'Tobacco and Cigarettes'. Many years ago, the shop was demolished and the building returned to its original use as a house only. *Malcolm Cant Collection.*

Mrs Murray's General Store

Mrs Murray's general store in Wheatfield Street was obviously a popular venue with Charlie Hoy in 1933 (back row, third from the left) and with many of his friends from neighbouring streets. Their 'angelic' faces suggest that they had nothing to do with the graffiti on the walls. The store seems to have been typical of small 'corner' shops of the day, but with an extra lucrative line of business, using the very latest technology: 'Mangling Done Here – by Electricity'. Mrs Murray is the lady on the right of the picture, instinctively wringing her hands.

Courtesy of Mrs May Hoy, née Strachan.

Courtesy of Mrs Louise Jenkins.

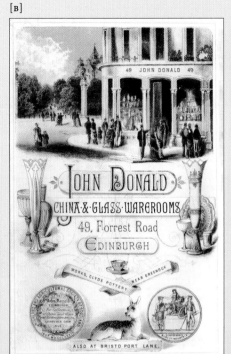

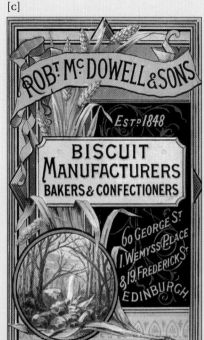

[A] Many businesses, such as the Cafe Royal Hotel and Frank G. Durrant, the ladies' tailor, were represented at the International Exhibition of Industry, Science and Art held on the Meadows in 1886.

[B] John Donald, the china and glass merchant, was at No. 49 Forrest Road and Bristo Port Lane when this advertisement was produced in the 1870s. The firm still trades from No. 10 Bristo Place.

[C] Robert McDowell & Sons, the biscuit manufacturer, was established in 1848 and had retail outlets in George Street, Wemyss Place and Frederick Street.

[D] Mackenzie & Mackenzie, Manufacturers to the Queen, produced Valetta Biscuits and many other products from their bakery in Broughton Road.

[E] Wiltshire Bacon, produced by Chas. & Thos. Harris & Co. Ltd, was sold by Robert Jardine, the provision merchant, of No. 8 Catherine Street, which formed part of Leith Street.

[A] Oakey's was famous for knife polish and blocks of black lead used to polish coal-fired ranges.

[B] By contrast, John Kelly & Son's advice in 1933 was to 'Scrap your old Range. It is Wasteful, Dirty and Unsightly' and instal their new 'Labsav' kitchen.

[C] Crystalade, the thirst-quenching drink, was one of the most popular products of T. & H. Smith & Co., of Canonmills and later Gorgie.

[D] T. Ruddiman Johnston, publishers of school maps and atlases supplied James Thin, Andrew Baxendine and many other booksellers throughout Scotland.

[E] In 1891, when this advertisement was produced, George Stewart & Co., of George Street, was listed as stationery and sealing wax manufacturers, printers and publishers.

[F] No self respecting cook was ever without Cox's Manual of Gelatine Cookery.
Courtesy of Jean Moffat.

Illustrations [A], [D] and [E]: © Edinburgh City Libraries. All rights reserved.

[A]

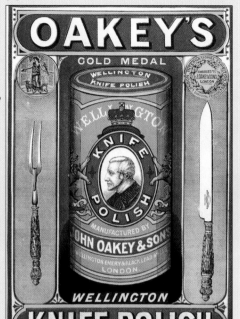

[B]

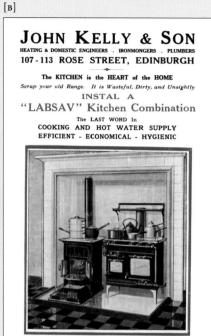

[C]

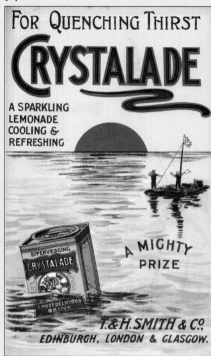

[D]

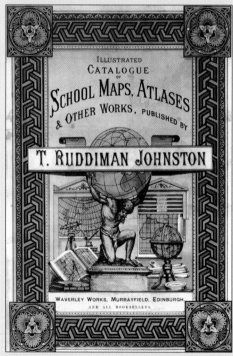

[E]

[F]

[A]

[B]

[C]

[A] This 1943 advertisement for McVitie & Price's biscuits features 'the boys' of No. 603 City of Edinburgh (Fighter) Squadron of the Auxiliary Air Force.

[B] Smith & Ritchie Ltd, like the page boy, was 'always at your service' from its Amphion Printing Works in Albert Street.

[C] The 1964 spring catalogue for W. Scott & Sons Ltd of Newington featured a wide variety of bulbs, roses and fruit trees with tips for best results. *Courtesy of Norman Scott.*

[A] St Cuthbert's Co-operative Association issued its own 'currency' in various denominations for use by customers in paying deliverymen who were not authorised to handle cash.

[B] St Cuthbert's issued small metal savings banks to encourage the idea of home-saving.

[C] Milk tokens were frequently left in the empty milk bottles, outside the door of the customer, ready for collection by the milkman.

[D] St Cuthbert's Co-operative Association Ltd logo for the centenary, 1859–1959.

[E] St Cuthbert's also had their own brand of soap made at the extensive factory at Shieldhall.

[F] A model of the four-in-hand coach, belonging to St Cuthbert's, used for ceremonial occasions.

[G] In 2005 the Society still urges the public to 'Become a Member of Scotmid'.

[H] The headquarters of the Scottish Midland Co-operative Society Ltd, formerly St Cuthbert's Co-operative Association, at No. 92 Fountainbridge, Edinburgh

[I] St Vincent Arrowroot was made for St Cuthbert's Co-operative at Shieldhall near Renfrew. It was mixed with milk to make a nutritious, filling pudding for young families.

All courtesy of Scottish Midland Co-operative Society Ltd.

[A]

[B]

[C]

[D]

[E]

[F]

[G]

[H]

[I]

28

PART 2: NON-FOOD SHOPS

Below. Mrs Kenmure's Apartments, No. 41 Broughton Street, photographed sometime between 1924 and 1931. George Keddie, Wine and Spirit Merchant, was at No. 39 and the shop on the left, beside the railings, was a confectioner's run by Mrs Martinelli. *Malcolm Cant Collection.*

Part 2 includes about ninety pictures of what could be loosely described as the 'non-food' shops. The photographs have again been arranged in groups, by trade, and are frequently corner shops serving small close-knit communities. Others, of course, moved on from humble beginnings as the firms prospered and were passed down 'from father, to son, to grandson', although it has to be said that the driving force behind the business was frequently the female side of the family. Some firms, like Lorimer & Beetham, House

Furnishers, at Churchhill and Wm Scott & Sons Ltd, Nurseymen, at Newington, became household names with a reputation throughout Scotland and beyond.

In addition to the photographs of specific shops, there are a few street scenes chosen to illustrate well-known parts of the City which have been completely redeveloped since the photographs were taken. The most notable examples are: the cluster of shops and houses which stood in Leven Street on the site now occupied by the King's Theatre; Tolbooth Wynd, in Leith, with every conceivable shop apparently doing a roaring trade; and a row of fairly small shops on Lindsay Place, demolished many years ago to make way for the long-awaited Museum of Scotland at the top of Chambers Street. Also included are one or two 'temporary' shops in the form of stands at the Scottish National Exhibition held at Saughton in 1908. Although many of the businesses were transient, others, like Ferguson's Rock, were in Edinburgh for many years before and after the Exhibition.

It is interesting to note, by modern standards, how many small shops were able to remain in business while restricting their stock to one main commodity (e.g. tobacconists, although they were frequently also stationers and newsagents).

As with Part 1, many of the images

THE WEE SHOP
The Wee Shop at No. 38 St John's Road, Corstorphine, in 1984. *Photograph by Andrew M. Broom. Courtesy of The Corstorphine Trust.*

include the proprietor and/or the staff standing outside the main door of the shop. Where identified, the names of the people have been included in the caption. Sadly, there are some where the identities have been lost or can only be surmised.

There are two groups of photographs which are not, strictly speaking, shops. The first group relates to the shorthand and typing institutions in Shandwick Place and North Charlotte Street, and the second group includes a few of Edinburgh's many fascinating public houses, like Paddy Crossan's in Rose Street, and the Bay Horse and Edinburgh Dock Bar in Leith.

One shop has a reputation out of all proportion to its size, namely, The Wee Shop at No. 38 St John's Road in Corstorphine. Thanks to the work done by The Corstorphine Heritage Centre, its description and history have been accurately recorded. It measures about 40" (1 metre) at its widest point (at the front door) and tapers to about 18" (45 cms) at the back, and is about 4' 6" (1.35m) deep. Originally it was the headquarters of the Corstorphine Temperance Society but in the 1970s ownership passed to The Corstorphine Trust. Over the years there have been several types of shop: in the 1940s, a tobacconist and confectioner run by Mr Thomson; a corsetry business run by Mrs Grundey from 1952 to 1959; Andrew Sives, the boot repairer; Mr Mason, a watchmaker; and an office for various coal merchants, including Macdonald, Bruce Lindsay and Brotchie. At the present day it is used by the solicitors, Dickson, McNiven & Dunn, W. S., to advertise property sales.

LEVEN STREET

The corner of Tarvit Street and Leven Street had several thriving retail outlets despite the buildings being in a rather dilapidated condition. The photograph was taken not long before the demolition of all the buildings for the construction of the King's Theatre in 1906. The corner premises were occupied by a branch of Covent Garden, Leith, selling strawberries, gooseberries and cut flowers. No. 2 Leven Street (below the advertisement for Thomson's Oatmeal) was occupied by T. J. Malcolmson, Grocer and Wine Merchant, and No. 4 by a gilder and restorer of paintings. The tall chimney, in the centre of the picture, is part of Drumdryan Brewery which was founded in 1760 and demolished in 1904. *Malcolm Cant Collection.*

TOLBOOTH WYND

When this photograph was taken in 1909, both sides of Tolbooth Wynd were lined with shops, selling all the main commodities and the fashion trends of the day. On the left, at No. 34, is David S. Stark, Tea, Wine and Spirit Merchants, which has special blends of Scotch Whisky advertised in the window. The large corner shop on the right, Nos. 31 & 33, was occupied by Joseph Hepworth & Sons, Wholesale and Retail Clothiers, which also had premises at No. 27 North Bridge and No. 53 Earl Grey Street. Other clothes' shops in Tolbooth Wynd included F. Mohan, Outfitter, at No. 35 and William Jeffrey & Son, Drapers, at Nos. 42-48. *Malcolm Cant Collection.*

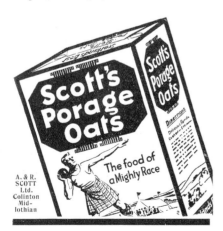

LINDSAY PLACE

The left-hand side of this 1956 photograph shows a line of shops in Lindsay Place, all of which were demolished for the construction of the Museum of Scotland at the top of Chambers Street. From left to right the shops are: Hewat of Edinburgh, Overall Specialists; James Lawrie & Son, Tobacconists; and Mason's Radio & Television. The No. 23 tram is about to turn right into Forrest Road and two-way traffic is also operating in Bristo Place. The original New North Free Church on the right of the picture is now used as the Bedlam Theatre.

RUSSELL'S OF THE MOUND

Thomas Russell, at No. 10 North Bank Street, specialised in trunks and portmanteaus, a wide selection of which can be seen laid out on the pavement. The wholesale and retail business also included brushes and baskets. The firm was on the Mound from at least 1846. In the 1940s and 1950s, No. 10 was occupied by the *Scottish Daily Express*, after which the old building was demolished, opening up the view of Lady Stair's House in the Close which runs up to the Lawnmarket. *Malcolm Cant Collection.*

TRUNK AND PORTMANTEAU ADVERTISMENTS

As can be seen from the accompanying advertisements, Russell's faced stiff competition from other long-established companies like Boswell's in Hanover Street, and Cleghorn's in George Street.

ROYAL PROMENADE, SCOTTISH NATIONAL EXHIBITION, 1908

The Scottish National Exhibition was held during the summer months of 1908 in the garden ground of Saughton Hall Mansion to the west of Balgreen Road, on land now used as Saughton Rose Garden and Saughton Public Park. The Exhibition attracted a wide range of interests, including Scottish industries, nursing, education, agriculture, bee keeping and artisan's work. The main entrance was from the corner of Gorgie Road and Balgreen Road where a new access bridge was built over the Water of Leith. A short driveway led to the Royal Promenade which ran almost the entire length of the site and opened into a rectangular arena bounded by the main exhibition buildings. The photograph shows a crowded Royal Promenade with the Ferguson's Rock Kiosk on the right. *Malcolm Cant Collection.*

ALEX FERGUSON'S KIOSK

Many of the business exhibits were very creative, notably Alex Ferguson's Kiosk advertising Edinburgh Rock. The upper part of the exhibit was intended to represent the City's coat-of-arms and the lower part, a rock temple. The firm was established in 1822. *Courtesy of Robin Sherman*

FERGUSON'S SHOP

Ferguson's Rock, manufactured at No. 1 Melbourne Place (part of George IV Bridge), is described on the face of the building as 'Safest Sweetmeats' but the window displays are hidden by drapes. *Malcolm Cant Collection.*

ALEXANDER FERGUSON,
CONFECTIONER
TO
H.M. the Queen and H.R.H. the Duke of Edinburgh,
1 MELBOURNE PLACE,
EDINBURGH.

All Confections
Manufactured or Sold by ALEXANDER FERGUSON are
WARRANTED GENUINE,

Vegetarian Restaurant

The Vegetarian Restaurant at the 1908 Exhibition proved to be a popular venue with sixpenny dinners and teas. *Malcolm Cant Collection.*

Lemco and Oxo Kiosk

This innovative kiosk was designed to appeal to patrons from throughout the United Kingdom and the world. The vertical board on the left lists London, Dublin, Birmingham, Bristol, Edinburgh, Glasgow, Hull, Liverpool, Manchester, Newcastle, Plymouth, Portsmouth and Sheffield: and the corresponding board on the right lists London, Antwerp, Berlin, Cologne, Hamburg, Milan, Paris, Bombay, Calcutta, Buenos Aires, Capetown and New York. Lemco was a popular meat extract sold in jars. *Courtesy of Robin Sherman.*

Cadbury's Stand

Cadbury's advertisement reads like an ordinary message on a picture postcard: 'Have just had and enjoyed a most delicious cup of Bournville Cocoa at Cadbury's pretty stand. Be sure you call at No. 103 Industrial Hall and try it for yourself'. *Malcolm Cant Collection.*

❧ JOHN NEIL, STATIONER

John Neil outside his stationery and tobacconist's shop at No. 242 Dalry Road in the 1920s.

❧ JOHN MENZIES & CO. LTD.

Menzies' bookstall in Waverley Station was always fully stocked with a wide range of newspapers, magazines and books, ideal for the travelling public. The bill boards include: Results of the Big Fight; and the Queen's Message to the Nation. In 1833, John Menzies started the company in modest premises 'up a few steps' at No. 61 Princes Street. According to the company history *The Making of John Menzies 1833-1983*, he acquired the Waverley Station site in 1862 which gave him the right to sell 'books, pamphlets and newspapers' every day except Sundays, between 6.15a.m. and 10.15p.m., provided that he did not sell any book 'objectionable in its moral character or tendency'. *Malcolm Cant Collection.*

❧ J. SIMPSON, NEWSAGENT & TOBACCONIST

John Simpson is recorded at No. 197 Easter Road from about 1913 until 1939, after which the proprietor was J. Meiklejohn who continued to use the original business name until 1962. In the photograph, the left-hand window is devoted to confectionery, with Cadbury's and Rowntree's Chocolates and Pastilles. The right-hand window has various cigarettes: Wills' Gold Flake; Prize Crop; and Capstan Navy Cut. The bill boards announce: Best Cup Final Pictures; British Flight over the North Pole; Bestway Books (with free dress patterns); and a Free Hand-Reading Offer. *Malcolm Cant Collection.*

ALEXANDER D. HUNTER, STATIONER

Alexander D. Hunter ran his newsagent's, stationer's and printer's business at No. 81 Bruntsfield Place from 1936, when he took over the previous business run by R. G. Bryan, until 1979 when he retired. Mr Hunter served an apprenticeship with Waterstons, the stationers, of George Street after which he went to Anderson's Arcade in Princes Street. He later moved to Jarrolds in Norwich but returned to Edinburgh in 1928 to set up as a stationer and newsagent, firstly in Clerk Street, and then at Bruntsfield. In addition to running the shop, Alexander Hunter was actively involved in the church, youth organisations, sport and, particularly, the history of Edinburgh. In the photograph there are advertisements for Wills' Woodbine cigarettes, Player's, and 'For Your Throat's Sake Smoke Craven 'A'. The bill boards are: Mr Thomas, Debate in Full; New Scottish Judge; Civil War Peril in China; Art in the School; Hawick and Selkirk Festivals; New Palais Des Nations; and Beat the Bookie, Wins 11-2. On the extreme right of the picture there is also a projecting sign indicating that the shop was an agent for Edinburgh Corporation Transport Parcel Express. *Courtesy of Mrs Pauline Matthews*

WILSON, CONFECTIONER AND TOBACCONIST

The photograph shows Mr Wilson, the proprietor, of the confectioner and tobacconist's business at No. 56 Gorgie Road, probably shortly before it was demolished in the 1930s. The building remains something of an enigma in view of its unusual construction: the bay window on the left looks like an addition to the original building; there is a hay-loft type opening above the window; and the shop frontage appears to be fitted into a high-arched doorway which could have been designed to house a carriage or motor vehicle. *Photograph by Mrs Nellie Denholm*

T. G. & A. M. Crocket, Drysalters

Nos. 190-194 Canongate were occupied by T. G. & A. M. Crocket as household furnishers and drysalters from the 1880s until 1935 when the business was taken over by Isaac Cairns. The various advertisements on the face of the building include Sunlight Soap, Venus Soap, Hudson's Soap and Colman's Starch. The entry at the left-hand side of the shop is St John's Close (No. 188) which led to Canongate Kilwinning Lodge at the back of the tenement. To the left again, the bracket light has the name, St John's Bar, and the fascia reads Wine & Spirit Merchant. The pub obviously took its name from St John's Street which is reached through the archway on the extreme left of the picture.
Malcolm Cant Collection.

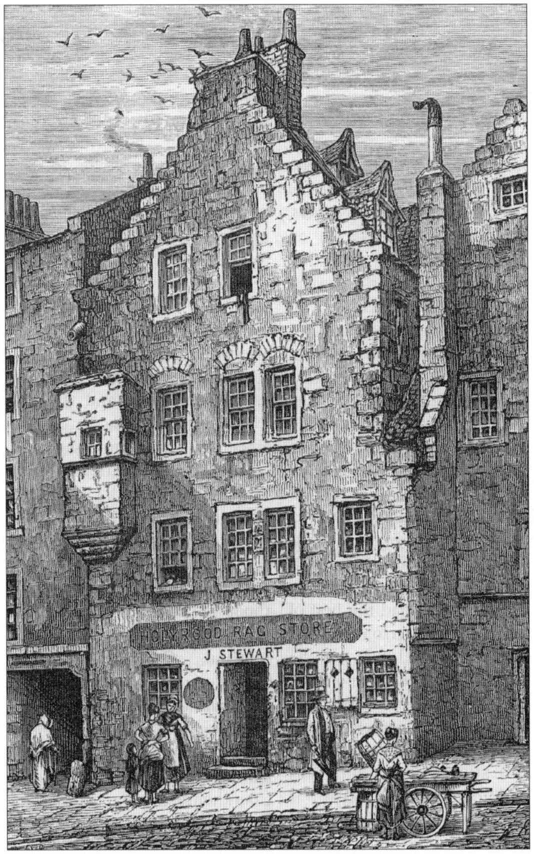

Stewart's Holyrood Rag Store

This once-grand building on the south side of the Canongate has been reduced to housing Mr J. Stewart's Holyrood Rag Store. According to *Grant's Old & New Edinburgh*, the building, erected in 1624, was the town mansion of the Nisbets of Dirleton, one of whom, Sir John Nisbet, was raised to the bench in 1664. Grant describes the unusual architectural feature on the left of the building as 'a square projecting turret, corbelled well out over the pavement' from which Sir John would, no doubt, have been able to see some of the citizens who were likely to appear before him. The etchings for Grant's *Old & New Edinburgh* were probably drawn in the late 1870s and the *Edinburgh & Leith Post Office Directory* for 1878-79 lists John Stewart as a general dealer at No. 82 Canongate.
From Grant's Old & New Edinburgh.

82-84 Canongate

By 1909 the town house of the Nisbets of Dirleton was better known as Nos. 82-84 Canongate which hosted a wonderful display of tin baths, pails, pots, pans, brushes, baskets and everything else that a good ironmonger would stock. Unfortunately, the name of the shop proprietor has not been traced. The entry on the right-hand side of the photograph is Strathie's Close and the one to the left of the ironmonger's is Reid's Close. To the left of Reid's Close is a much smaller shop, No.78, which changed hands frequently but was occupied by Charles H. McKenzie, a grocer, when the photograph was taken.
Malcolm Cant Collection.

FLEMING'S STORES

For many years Fleming's Stores was a very familiar part of Tollcross, the main shop being on the corner of Earl Grey Street and West Tollcross. James Fleming started in business as a hardware, smallware and fancy goods merchant, *c.* 1896, at No. 34 Earl Grey Street and No. 121 Fountainbridge. He moved to the corner premises, part of the Central Hall, in 1902. Later, other shops were established at No. 44 Home Street and No. 259 St John's Road, Corstorphine. In 1964 the Earl Grey Street shop was closed and the business was transferred to Lochrin Terrace which had previously been a store. In 1968 Fleming's ceased trading altogether.

J. MCKENZIE, TINSMITH & IRONMONGER

The large corner premises at No. 90 Gorgie Road, on the east corner with McLeod Street, were occupied in 1932 by J. McKenzie, Manufacturing Tinsmith & General Ironmongery. The windows, doorway and shop floor are crammed with all manner of household items: brushes, baskets, garden poles, cut leather and straps, Persil washing powder, stepladders and carpet beaters.

WM. K. WHITE, IRONMONGER

William K. White, Wholesale and Retail Ironmongers, established in 1834, had extensive premises, Nos. 121-129, on the north side of the High Street a few doors down from the junction with North Bridge. The photograph is taken from the visiting card of one of the firm's agents. The reverse side says: 'Mr Wm. K. White begs to inform you that his representative, Mr Andrew White, will have the pleasure of calling upon you on ... WEDNESDAY FIRST, when the favour of your orders will be esteemed and have careful attention'. *Courtesy of A. W. Brotchie.*

J. B. Watson, Optician & Photographic Dealer

J. B. Watson, the Optician, opened his first shop at No. 13 Shandwick Place in the early 1900s, in premises previously used by Thomas Haddow and Lizars, both of whom were also opticians. J. B. Watson later expanded into No. 15 and also opened a second shop at No. 3 Frederick Street in 1917. This advertisement comes from the cover of Watson's small photograph wallets which were in use from at least 1940.

The left-hand illustration shows the Shandwick Place premises in proximity to the West End clock, and the right-hand illustration shows the Frederick Street premises with a policeman directing traffic at the junction with Princes Street.
Courtesy of Mrs Patricia Davidson.

J. B. Watson obviously faced stiff competition from other opticians, notably George Prescott & Co. of No. 98 Lothian Road.

DUNCAN, FLOCKHART & CO., CHEMISTS, NORTH BRIDGE

John Duncan, the founder of Duncan, Flockhart & Co., was born on 26 August 1780 in Kinross. In 1794 he was apprenticed to a druggist in the Lawnmarket, Edinburgh for five years, after which he went to London. On returning from London in 1806 he opened his first shop in Perth. The illustration shows his first shop in Edinburgh, opened *c.* 1820, at No. 52 North Bridge. One of the first apprentices at North Bridge was the young and energetic William Flockhart who became a partner in 1832. By 1946 Duncan, Flockhart & Co. was employing about 200 staff, but in 1952 the firm was acquired by T. & H. Smith of Gorgie.
From The History of Duncan, Flockhart & Co.

DUNCAN, FLOCKHART & CO., CHEMISTS, PRINCES STREET

In 1846 a new branch of Duncan, Flockhart & Co. was opened at No. 39 Princes Street. The first apprentice was James Buchanan who became a partner in 1863 and moved to the North Bridge shop in 1865 where he remained until his retirement in 1904 at the age of 73. James Buchanan died in 1909, leaving a wife and several children living in Oswald House (in the Grange district) which had been built for them in 1876, to designs by the architect, Robert Morham. The last surviving daughter, Margaret Buchanan, died in 1988. The illustration shows the interior of Duncan Flockhart's shop at No. 39 Princes Street, fitted out with glass-covered cases, stacks of drawers, and open shelves with a display of the potions of the day. The firm also supplied the chloroform for Dr Simpson's historic experiment on 4 November 1847 when he succeeded in putting himself, and others, to sleep in the dining room of his house at No. 52 Queen Street. Having survived the 'controlled' experiment he went on to pioneer the use of chloroform for surgical operations and childbirth. Duncan Flockhart's factory and laboratories were at Holyrood Road (near the present-day Our Dynamic Earth) where the main products were chloroform and ether. There was also a drug-growing farm at Warriston, started around the time of the First World War.
From The History of Duncan, Flockhart & Co.

James Aikman & Sons, Wholesale Shoe Factors

The driver and delivery van were photographed outside the premises of James Aikman & Sons, Wholesale Shoe Factors, in Jeffrey Street. Aikman's was at Jeffrey Street from around 1891 when it was described as Leather & Boot Factors. Prior to that, it was at Niddry Street, a few doors away from A. D. Aikman, Leather Merchants. The Aikman family were also involved in the leather and boot industry at an address in the Lawnmarket, the earliest reference being, 'A. Aikman, shoemaker, at the head of the Lawnmarket', in 1810. *Malcolm Cant Collection.*

Apex Shoe Co.

The Apex supply stores for boots, shoes and waterproofs was at Nos 1 & 2 Chambers Street from around 1914. Later it extended round the corner to include No. 74 South Bridge until 1933 when the premises became part of J. & R. Allan's expanding empire in South Bridge. The upper windows in Chambers Street and South Bridge are those of Thomas Rankine & Sons, Boot Factors, who later moved to No. 22 St James' Square. *Malcolm Cant Collection.*

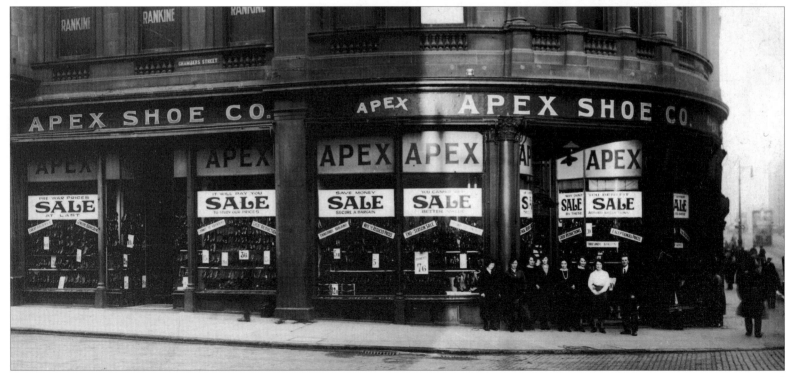

J. Carse & Son, Boot & Shoe Maker

John Carse, the bootmaker, was operating from No. 26a Barony Street from 1905 to 1937. The firm became J. Carse & Son in 1923 which suggests that the photograph was taken sometime between 1923 and 1937. *Courtesy of Margeorie Mekie.*

Wauxwell Shoe Company

In 1903 John Rae was the manager of the British American Boot Stores at No. 16 Hanover Street. He retained the position of manager when the firm was renamed the Wauxwell Shoe Company a year or so later. The company remained in the same premises until 1956 after which the shop was occupied by James Allan & Son Ltd, the footwear specialists. Wauxwell's advertisements claimed that: 'the problem of supplying a comfortable, well-fitting and durable boot or shoe at a moderate price has been solved by the Wauxwell Shoe Coy. on their new system of manufacturing and stocking boots and shoes at their stores': proof, indeed, if proof were needed, that anyone who visits Wauxwell, walks well! The upper picture, *c.* 1904, shows the exterior of the shop in Hanover Street, and the lower picture, the interior. *Courtesy of Margeorie Mekie.*

JAMES ALLAN & SON LTD, FOOTWEAR SPECIALISTS

James Allan & Son Ltd, established in 1783, had branches at No. 123 Princes Street and No. 42 Leith Street, as well as in Glasgow and Dundee. Allan's Foot Service included everything associated with footwear 'from the Infant's first Silk Shoes to the Field Marshal's Jack Boots'. Surgical boots were made to measure and all kinds of special appliances were developed for people with foot problems. The firm's advertisements in the 1930s included 'Lovely Designs for Ladies' Afternoon and Evening Shoes, with Silk Stockings to blend in great variety of shades'.

JAMES ALLAN & SON LTD ADVERTISEMENTS

'Makers of Boots and Shoes For Every Occasion'.

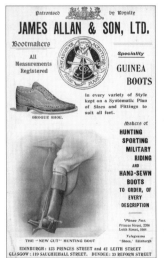

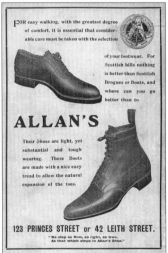

STOCKBRIDGE, EDINBURGH.

The Clock, Morningside Road, Edinburgh.

ARNOLD SEFTOR, FURRIER

Bertram Seftor, born in London, came to Edinburgh around 1910 and worked for a while with Russ & Winkler, the famous Edinburgh furriers, in Princes Street. In 1914, when Bertram was twenty-four years of age, he opened his first shop at No. 9 Gillespie Place, which, unfortunately, had to be closed shortly thereafter at the outbreak of the First World War. When Bertram was discharged from the army at the end of the war, he re-opened the shop and started to rebuild the business. He opened a salon in Glasgow and moved his family there, while maintaining the Edinburgh shop. The experiment was short-lived, however, as he returned to Edinburgh a few years later and opened bigger premises at Nos 97 & 99 Shandwick Place. Bertram Seftor's son, Arnold, joined the firm in 1932 at the age of sixteen and became the managing director in 1942 after his father died. After the Second World War, Arnold decided to secure new premises and set up business in his own name. After a delay of some months, premises at No. 1 Marchmont Crescent were bought. These required considerable renovation following war-time bomb damage. Arnold Seftor, Furrier, was established at the Marchmont premises in 1946 when Arnold's wife, Renée, joined the firm. The third generation of the family, Brian Seftor, joined the firm in 1964 and now runs the business with the assistance of his mother and his wife, Moira, who joined the firm in 1972. The photograph shows the premises at the corner of Marchmont Crescent and Marchmont Road in 1965. *Courtesy of the Seftor family. Photograph by J. Kinghorn.*

ARNOLD SEFTOR, FURRIER

Mrs Arnold Seftor in the Marchmont showroom in 1965. *Courtesy of the Seftor family. Photograph by J. Kinghorn.*

ARNOLD SEFTOR, FURRIER

Seftor's advertising material, depicting their clientele at the Marchmont showroom in 1965. *Courtesy of the Seftor family.*

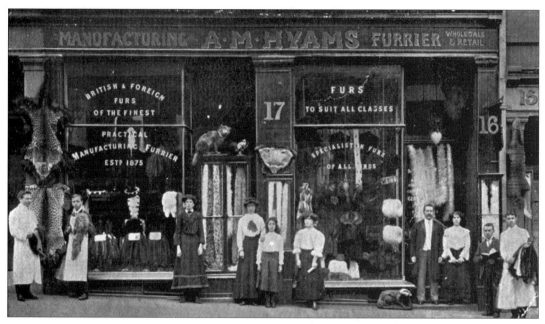

HYAMS, FURRIER

Abraham Hyams started in business as a furrier in 1898 in fairly modest premises at No. 6 Brighton Street. A few years later the business address was No. 48 Lothian Street but as Brighton Street was absorbed into Lothian Street around that time, it is possible that the two addresses refer to the same property. Mr Hyams moved to No. 16 Bruntsfield Place in 1905 and later opened branches in George Street, Edinburgh, Union Street, Aberdeen and Great Western Road, Glasgow. The firm was renamed A. M. Hyams & Sons Ltd in 1922 and later took the general trade name Hyams of Bruntsfield. Hyams greatly extended the premises and remained there until 1956. Other members of the Hyams family were also furriers on the south side of Edinburgh. The photograph shows a large staff and well-dressed windows at Nos. 16 & 17 Bruntsfield Place, presumably sometime between 1905 and 1922 when the firm became a limited company. Although the window signage declares that the business was established in 1875, no trace has been found of where the first premises were situated. *Malcolm Cant Collection.*

J. KARTER & COMPANY, FURRIERS

J. Karter & Company, Manufacturing Furriers, was established in 1926 at No. 72 George Street, on the west corner with Frederick Street. It also had retail outlets in Piccadilly, London, and Sauchiehall Street, Glasgow. The advertisement shows a drawing of the Edinburgh shop front as it would have looked in 1927 with a few models included to set the scene. Karter remained at No. 72 until around 1951 after which it appears to have suspended retail sales in Edinburgh. In 1954 the firm reappeared as J. Karter & Company (Furs) Ltd. at No. 130 Lothian Road (part of the Lothian House complex) where it remained until 1959. *Malcolm Cant Collection.*

✌ Robert Cresser, Brush Shop

When this photograph was taken *c.* 1958 by James L. A. Evatt, Cresser's brush shop at No. 40 Victoria Street had been in business for many years, albeit at different addresses, including No. 345 High Street and No. 40 St Mary's Street.

✌ Alexander Mackie's Tool Shop

Below left. Alexander Mackie established his first tool shop in 1875 at No. 4 Victoria Street from which he sold a wide selection of tools for use by amateurs and tradesmen, in addition to ironmongery, lathes and shop fittings.

✌ Alexander Mackie's Tool & Cutlery Warehouse

Below right. Additional premises were opened by Alexander Mackie in 1882 at No. 8 Melbourne Place, part of George IV Bridge. His advertising material included a bewildering selection of goods 'to meet all tastes and the requirements of every age and station in life'. The list included: cutlery, toast racks, jelly dishes, electro-plate, optical goods (spectacles, eye-glasses, telescopes, thermometers and barometers), watches, clocks, fishing tackle (including artificial minnows), golf clubs, guns, revolvers, drawing instruments, scientific novelties, model engines, dog collars, whistles, cycle lamps, bells, telephones, medical coils, magic lanterns and cameras. Guns and revolvers included 'breech and muzzle loading guns, rook rifles, walking stick guns, ammunition, and the patent air gun which shoots balls and darts, and can be used equally well for indoor and outdoor amusement as it is capable of killing birds, rabbits, etc.'

❧ MURRAY'S TOOLSTORE, NO. 4 DALRY ROAD

Left. The Murray family has run tool shops at five separate locations in Edinburgh since 1942. In the early years of the Second World War, Alexander Murray and his wife, Winifred, lived in Southampton where they ran a garage and a restaurant. When the business premises and their house were all destroyed by enemy action in 1941, they came north to Edinburgh with their four children. The family, and everything that they possessed, fitted quite easily into a small Humber car for the journey. On arrival in Edinburgh, Mr Murray obtained the tenancy of vacant premises at No. 4 Dalry Road where he opened his first shop selling second-hand tools which had been saved when the garage was bombed. Initially, the shop was run by Winifred while Alexander worked in a local garage. Despite the austerity of the war years and the late 1940s, Dalry was a good place in which to open a tool shop as there were so many large firms employing joiners, cabinetmakers, engineers and mechanics. Three sons of the family, Ian, Fred and Scott, followed their father into the business which is still operating at Morrison Street and South Clerk Street. The photograph shows Ian Murray, on the left, and Fred Murray, on the right, outside the first shop at No. 4 Dalry Road in 1948.

❧ MURRAY'S TOOLSTORE, NO. 11 DALRY ROAD

Centre left. The second shop, opened in 1957 at No. 11 Dalry Road, operated until 1999 when the business transacted there was transferred to the nearest branch at No. 83 Morrison Street.

❧ MURRAY'S TOOLSTORE, NO. 83 MORRISON STREET

Lower left. The Morrison Street premises were opened in 1969 and are still operating.

❧ MURRAY'S TOOLSTORE, NO. 84 SOUTH CLERK STREET

Far left. The South Clerk Street shop, still operating, was opened in 1965 after the closure of the nearby branch at Bristo Street.

Photographs courtesy of Fred Murray.

JOHN HENRY, JEWELLER

Queen Mary, cheered by a small group of enthusiastic well-wishers, leaves John Henry's jeweller's shop at Earl of Moubray House, No. 51 High Street. There was also a branch at No. 183 Canongate, conveniently named Holyrood House – presumably to differentiate it from the main retail outlet at Moubray House.
Malcolm Cant Collection.

PATRONISED BY H.M. THE QUEEN AND
H.R.H. THE PRINCE OF WALES

JOHN HENRY

OLD SHEFFIELD PLATE
CHINA, OLD ENGLISH
& FRENCH FURNITURE
AND FINE JEWELS

EARL OF MOUBRAY HOUSE
51 HIGH STREET, EDINBURGH
Also at 85 & 87 High St., Edinburgh

Closed on Saturdays at 1 p.m.

Cablegrams: "Moubray, Edinburgh." Phone 24580
Goods shipped to all parts of the world

GORGIE HAIRDRESSING SALOON

J. Mitchell's combined hairdresser's and tobacconist's shop was at No. 267 Gorgie Road, on the south side of the road near the junction with Robertson Avenue. When this photograph was taken the window display was entirely devoted to *Smart Fiction*. This weekly periodical was published in London between 1913 and 1924 and ran to 614 issues before being incorporated into *Smart Novels*. The issue prominently displayed in the window bears the legend 'The World of Sin', while billboards advertise other sensational sounding stories, including 'Her Honour at Stake' and 'The Soul of an Outcast'. *Malcolm Cant Collection.*

MAISON TENSFELDT, HAIR EXPERTS

If *Smart Fiction* was not enough to curl your hair, there was always Maison Tensfeldt's permanent waving, available from their salon at No. 137 Princes Street. This advertisement clearly refers to Maison Tensfeldt at the Princes Street salon, but other advertisements refer to Madame Tensfeldt, the hair and complexion expert at Princes Street and Maison Tensfeldt, the hair specialist and wig maker at Nos. 79-81 Shandwick Place. Clearly the Tensfeldt family was an integral part of the hairdressing world in Edinburgh during the first half of the twentieth century. This advertisement is dated *c.* 1927.

JOHN F. McGREGOR, WATCHMAKER & JEWELLER

This undated photograph shows John F. McGregor (in the centre) outside his jeweller's shop at No. 86 Morningside Road where the firm was established in 1900. At the end of the First World War, Mr McGregor also opened premises at No. 72 Princes Street, described as 'on the first floor' which presumably precluded him from having a display window onto what was then Edinburgh's principal shopping area. The experiment does not appear to have lasted long, however, as by the mid-1920s Mr McGregor had moved to No. 22 Morningside Road where he remained until 1957.
Malcolm Cant Collection.

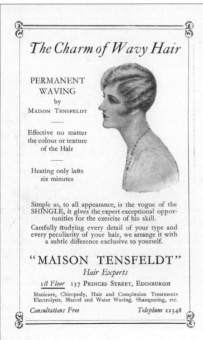

The Charm of Wavy Hair

PERMANENT
WAVING
by
MAISON TENSFELDT

Effective no matter
the colour or texture
of the Hair

Heating only lasts
six minutes

Simple as, to all appearance, is the vogue of the SHINGLE, it gives the expert exceptional opportunities for the exercise of his skill.
Carefully studying every detail of your type and every peculiarity of your hair, we arrange it with a subtle difference exclusive to yourself.

"MAISON TENSFELDT"
Hair Experts
1st Floor 137 PRINCES STREET, EDINBURGH
Manicure, Chiropody, Hair and Complexion Treatments
Electrolysis, Marcel and Water Waving, Shampooing, etc.

Consultations Free   Telephone 22348

❧ M. Gibson, Drapery & Smallwares

John Skinner & Co., drapers & clothiers, occupied
No. 7 Barony Street from 1900 to 1927, after which
they moved to larger premises at No. 28 Dublin
Street. In 1928 the shop in Barony Street was taken
over by Mrs M. Gibson who ran it for a few years
only as a drapery and smallgoods store.
Courtesy of A. W. Brotchie.

❧ George McCrae, Hatter

George McCrae ran a very successful business as a
hatter from No. 37 Cockburn Street. Established in
1880 with the motto 'Competition Defied', the shop
had an unrivalled stock of hosiery, scarfs, ties, gloves,
hats, cuffs, collars and umbrellas. Among the most
popular items were: the 2/11d hat – 'a good felt hat,
wearable and durable for working men'; and the 1/-
(5p) scarf 'looked upon by Edinburgh people as a
marvel of cheapness and quality in every shape and
pattern'. In addition to running the business, George
McCrae was actively involved in public life: he was a
captain in the Fourth Volunteer Battalion Royal Scots,
and held a number of political appointments. The
illustration shows what must have been one of the
most distinctive parcel delivery vans in the city. To
the tip of the big hat it was nearly ten feet high and
the driver was decked out with a red coat, white
breeches, top boots and a livery hat with a bold band.
The ilustration is dated *c*. 1890. *From Scotland of
Today:* © *Edinburgh City Libraries. All rights reserved.*

J. R. Ross, Cycles

James R. Ross and his daughter, Lottie, outside the family cycle repair shop at No. 259 Dalry Road, *c.* 1940. *Courtesy of Mrs Lottie Morrice, née Ross.*

Robert Robertson, Cycles

Robert Robertson and his youngest son, Tam, outside the family cycle repair shop in St Stephen's Street, *c.* 1926. *Courtesy of Mrs Lottie Morrice, née Ross.*

Ernest Kohler & Son, Musical Instrument makers

Not many shops in Edinburgh, even in 1904 when this photograph was taken, received deliveries of violin wood. This consignment has just been delivered to the premises of Ernest Kohler & Son, Music Instrument Makers, at No. 101 Leith Street. The firm was established as harp-string makers in 1800 in the Old Town. Early addresses included No. 59 Leith Wynd (off the Canongate), No. 54 St Mary's Wynd, and No. 187 High Street. By the middle of the nineteenth century, Kohler was at No. 21 North Bridge where it remained until 1897. Thereafter the retail shop was at No. 101 Leith Street and the store and workshop was at No. 117. Finally, it moved to No. 5 Blenheim Place in 1935 until the early 1950s when the shop closed. *Courtesy of Margeorie Mekie.*

❧ HAYMARKET LIBRARY

The Haymarket Library was situated on the corner of Rosebery Crescent and Clifton Terrace, almost opposite Haymarket Station. It was at No. 15 Clifton Terrace for a very short time only, between 1906 and 1910, during which time it was run by Alexander & Pearson which were also stationers and newsagents. *Courtesy of Robin Sherman.*

❧ GRANT'S BOOKSHOP

The photograph comes from an advertisement, dated 1894, giving full details of lending charges made by R. Grant & Son who had been in business in Edinburgh since 1804.

❧ NAPIERS, PICTURE FRAMERS AND GILDERS

Douglas M. W. Napier, aged two, in 1924 outside his father's shop at Nos 25 & 26 Bruntsfield Place. Robert W. Napier, FRSA, MSP, was the sole proprietor of R. & R. Napier, Picture Framers, Carvers and Gilders and author of *John Thomson of Duddingston*, published in 1919 by Oliver & Boyd of Tweeddale Court. *Courtesy of Mrs Jean Napier.*

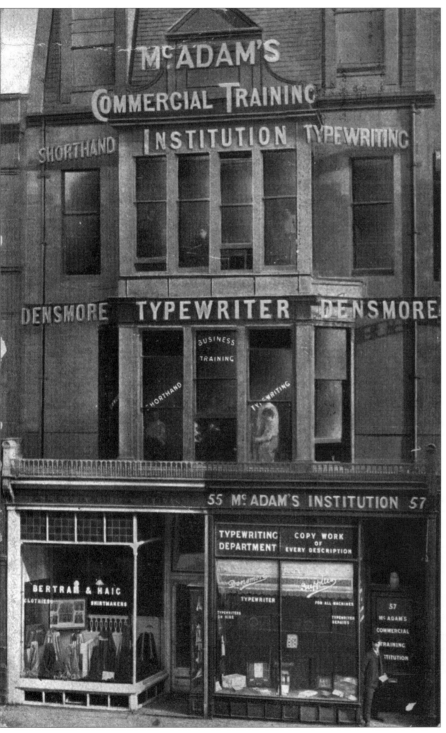

McAdam's Commercial Training Institution

In 1906, when the photograph was taken, McAdam's Commercial Training Institution occupied extensive premises at Nos. 55 & 57 Shandwick Place where it ran courses in shorthand writing, typing and general business training. A surviving invitation card from the same period shows that it was not all work and no play: 'Mr & Mrs McAdam hope to have the pleasure of your company at the Institution "At Home" to be held in the Edinburgh Cafe Co. on Friday evening 29th June at 7 o'clock. 57 Shandwick Place. RSVP.' The Edinburgh Cafe Co. was a very popular meeting place and is illustrated on page 23. The Commercial Training Institution later moved to Nos 5 & 6 North Charlotte Street where it continued in business for several decades. *Malcolm Cant Collection.*

A wistful look in a quiet, unidentified, bustle-free office.

❧ DAVID CLARK, WINE & SPIRIT MERCHANT
Outside Clark's Bar at No. 80 Lauriston Place, the
bar staff, a few regulars and some children are
fascinated by the horse-drawn fire engine returning
to the Central Fire Station at the head of Lady
Lawson Street. The cloud of steam is not coming
from the horses but from the water pump at the
back of the tender. David Clark also ran the Cattle
Market Hotel from No. 80 Lauriston Place, the
name being taken from the nearby market and
slaughterhouse. The Central Fire Station was built
on the site of the Lauriston cattle market in 1900.
Courtesy of Pat Scoular.

❧ VOLUNTEER ARMS, MORNINGSIDE ROAD
Below and below right. Morningside's village inn,
dating from the early nineteenth century, stands on
the south corner of Canaan Lane and Morningside
Road. Originally known as the Volunteers' Rest, or
The Rifleman, it later changed its name to The
Volunteer Arms or The Canny Man's. At the end of
the eighteenth century it was a small single-storey
building resembling a cottage which was purchased
by James Kerr in 1871. The present handsome two-
storey building on the same site is still in the hands
of the Kerr family. *Malcolm Cant Collection.*

Photograph by Phyllis M. Cant.

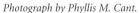

THE BAY HORSE, WINES & SPIRITS

The Bay Horse, under the management of C. G. Lane, was at Nos 63 & 65 Henderson Street, Leith. *Malcolm Cant Collection.*

EDINBURGH DOCK BAR

The Edinburgh Dock Bar, on the corner of Bath Road and Salamander Street, was run by John T. Ritchie in the early 1900s. It took its name from the Edinburgh Dock, opened in 1881 as part of the extended Port of Leith. The large group of children and adults in the street and at the windows were brought together for a celebratory photograph to thank John Ritchie for providing free dinners for the children during one of the pre-1920 dock strikes. *Courtesy of Mrs Patricia Davidson.*

PADDY'S BAR

A typical scene of comfort and relaxation in Paddy's Bar at No. 49 Rose Street in the 1950s. The bar was named after Paddy Crossan, the well-known Hearts footballer. Patrick James Crossan, who came from Addiewell, played for Hearts between 1911 and 1925, and died on 29 April 1933. The bar's wide selection of beers and spirits, and its open coal fire in the winter, made it a popular venue for regulars and visitors alike. *Malcolm Cant Collection.*

LORIMER & BEETHAM, DRAPERS & HOUSE FURNISHERS

Right. The partnership of Lorimer & Beetham was formed between Robert Lorimer and Frederick Beetham in 1946 when Mr Lorimer responded to Mr Beetham's press advertisement seeking a partner for a new furniture shop. At the time, Robert Lorimer was working in an insurance office in Edinburgh but was looking for a new challenge in which to invest his 'demob money'. Their first premises were at No. 63 Morningside Road. Within ten years, No. 61 Morningside Road had been acquired along with No. 7 Church Hill Place. When Frederick Beetham died suddenly in 1960, the Lorimer family formed a limited company and continued to expand the firm. By the late 1960s they had consolidated their position on Morningside Road, and had also acquired Nos 7–21 Church Hill Place. Robert Lorimer's family also entered the business, Lindsay as a chartered accountant, and Shelagh, trained in interior design. Over the years, the Lorimer family built up a substantial retail business as well as numerous contracts throughout Scotland for hotels, churches and golf clubs. The photograph shows the original shop at No. 63 Morningside Road, in 1950, at the time of the 4th Birthday Sale.

LORIMER & BEETHAM, DRAPERS & HOUSE FURNISHERS

Above far right. This mid-1960s photograph shows Lorimer & Beetham well on its way to occupying most of the block in Morningside Road.

LORIMER & BEETHAM, DRAPERS & HOUSE FURNISHERS

Right. Lorimer & Beetham was in Church Hill Place from 1955 but it was not until the late 1960s that it took over additional shops, seen here receiving a final coat of paint before opening. *Photographs courtesy of the Lorimer family.*

❧ W. SCOTT & SONS LTD, NURSERYMEN

Left. The business of W. Scott & Sons, Nurserymen, Florists and Seedsmen, operated in the Newington area for almost forty years. The firm was established at No. 59 Newington Road in 1949 by William Scott who was joined by his elder son, William Lawson Scott, shortly thereafter. Before setting up in business, William Scott had gained experience as a foreman with Robert Weddell & Son, Gardeners and Florists, of No. 18a Suffolk Road, on ground belonging to the Lord Gilmour Trust. In 1949 William Scott brought his fourth son, Norman, into the business which became W. Scott & Sons Ltd in 1962. During the 1950s, the business expanded rapidly: in 1953 No. 61 Newington Road was acquired and the basement premises of No. 1 West Newington Place became the main retail outlet for plants and sundries; and in 1957 Nos. 53 and 55 Newington Road were bought to create Scott's Garden Centre. The photograph shows Norman Scott in 1955 outside the premises at Nos 59 & 61 beside his brand new Austin A40 van with the Interflora logo on the door. *Courtesy of Norman Scott.*

❧ W. SCOTT & SONS LTD, NURSERYMEN

Above, far left. Scott's built up a very varied trade with a floral department at Newington Road catering for the many banks and insurance companies, as well as wreaths for the main funeral directors. Thousands of bulbs were imported from Holland for the Christmas trade, and trees and shrubs from Belgium for general sale. Scott's also acted as wholesalers for Woolworths, Stewart's in North St Andrew Street, and Dobbie's and Downie's in Shandwick Place. Unfortunately, Scott's lease at Suffolk Road (previously used by Weddell) was not renewed in 1969, which meant that the garden ground of No. 53 Newington Road had to be used for stocking plants. One of the last major property acquisitions was in 1978 when No. 58 Newington Road was opened as a hardware shop. By the early 1980s, independent, family-run garden centres were beginning to feel the effects of competition from bulk buyers like Dodge City which required the likes of Scott's to specialise in more unusual plants and shrubs. Scott's eventually closed in 1988, four years after the death of the founder, William Scott. *Courtesy of Norman Scott.*

❧ JOHN M. COMRIE LTD, GARDEN CENTRE

Above. John M. Comrie and his daughter, Betty, outside the family business on the corner of Colinton Road and Bruntsfield Place in 1957. The nursery and florists was taken over by John M. Comrie in 1928. *Courtesy of Mrs Betty Cunningham, née Comrie.*

❧ MULHEARN & BROTCHIE, GARDEN CENTRE

Above. Comrie's Garden Centre was acquired by Mulhearn & Brotchie *c.* 1962 and greatly extended over the years. It closed in 2005 in anticipation of a proposed redevelopment of the site. *Photograph by Phyllis M. Cant.*

LEVEN STREET POST OFFICE

Right. Leven Street Post Office was run by John Bayne at No. 44 Leven Street at the end of the nineteenth century and into the twentieth century. The post office business was combined with that of a bookseller and stationer which had previously been at No. 13 Leven Street. In the late 1920s the post office was moved again to the other side of the road at No. 9 Gillespie Place. The photograph, which shows the post office on the corner of Leven Street and Glengyle Terrace, is probably dated *c.* 1905 when the shop to the left was occupied by William Dickson, Corn Merchant.
Courtesy of Robin Sherman.

GENERAL POST OFFICE, WATERLOO PLACE

Below right. The General Post Office at the East End was built in the 1860s to designs by the architect, Robert Matheson, on the site of Shakespeare Square and the old Theatre Royal. It has been greatly altered on several occasions from the original design. *Malcolm Cant Collection.*

COMELY BANK POST OFFICE

Below. The photograph is taken from a postcard sent by 'AMD' to a Miss Leslie of Kingussie on 26 October 1908. Comely Bank Post Office at No. 10 Comely Bank Avenue was run by the Misses J. & M. Glen whose names are on the front window. There is an advertisement above the door for Paton's Alloa knitting wools, as well as a post office notice which lists the classes of business transacted: money orders, savings bank, parcel post, insurance and annuity.

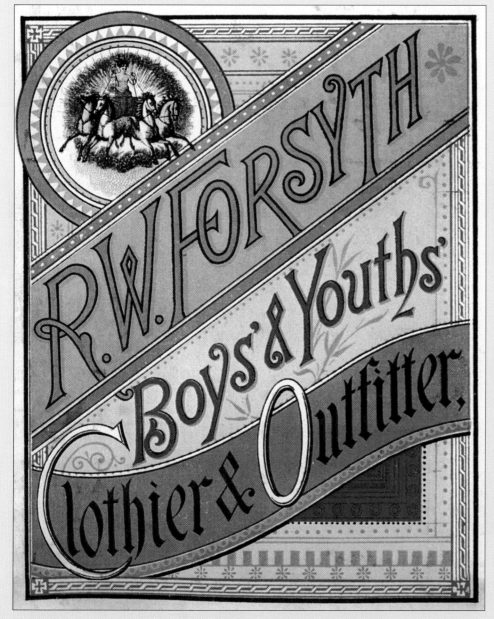

[A] and [B] R. W. Forsyth, Clothier and Outfitter, had premises in Princes Street, Edinburgh, as well as in Glasgow and London. The Edinburgh store closed in 1981.

[A]

[B]

[C]

[A] Jenner's advertising material frequently stated the obvious: that the store was 'the most fashionable shopping centre in Scotland'. *Malcolm Cant Collection.*

[B] The front cover of Jenner's sales brochure for 1940 depicted 'The Gay Companions' range by Pringle Sportswear. *© Edinburgh City Libraries. All rights reserved.*

[C] Kennington & Jenner, complete with colourful blinds, in the original premises on the corner of Princes Street and South St David's Street. *Courtesy of Jenners.*

[A]

[C]

[B]

[D]

[A] The advertisement, *c.* 1903, celebrates the amalgamation of James Gray & Son, ironmongers, and Smiths & Company, purveyors of lamps and oils, in their new premises at No. 89 George Street. *Courtesy of James Gray & Son.*

[B] J. & R. Allan, the drapers, announce new deliveries of their spring and summer novelties at their extensive premises on South Bridge. © *Edinburgh City Libraries. All rights reserved.*

[C] and [D] Elegance and sophistication were self-evident at Russ & Winkler, Edinburgh's premier furrier which was at No. 132 Princes Street from 1884 until 1958.

[A] The Thomson family's first Edinburgh shop was in Shandwick Place in 1845. Later the business moved to South Bridge and then North Bridge. It became Arnott's in 1976 and closed in 1981.

[B] This 1956 advertisement marked the opening of Wylie & Lochhead's new store and Epicure Restaurant at No. 25 Shandwick Place.

[C] Hamilton & Inches, Goldsmiths, Silversmiths, Jewellers and Watchmakers, was established in 1866 by James Hamilton and his nephew, Robert Kirk Inches, at No. 90a Princes Street. The firm still operates from No. 87 George Street. *Courtesy of Hamilton & Inches.*

[A]

"PATRICK THOMSON. LTD.

SETS THE BALL OF FASHION ROLLING.

PATRICK THOMSON, LTD *Cash Drapery Stores* NORTH BRIDGE. EDINBURGH.

Hamilton & Inches

Gold and Silversmiths, Jewellers, Watch and Clockmakers

87 George Street, Edinburgh EH2 3EY Telephone: 031-225 4898

Three hundred years after the granting of the Royal Charter
by King James VII of Scotland,
the craft of goldsmithing and silversmithing still continues
and flourishes in the heart of Edinburgh.
Our congratulations to the Incorporation of Goldsmiths of the City of Edinburgh.

[C]

[B]

WYLIE & LOCHHEAD LTD

Adjacent to Princes Street and the Caledonian Hotel, and only a few minutes' walk from Haymarket Station, with the popular Epicure Restaurant adjoining and car parking facilities nearby, Wylie & Lochhead's New Store is most conveniently situated.

The Entrance and Reception Hall reflect a well-balanced blending of Period furnishing within an atmosphere of modern decor and lighting—an expression itself of good design and colour sense.

EDINBURGH'S NEW STORE · · ·

At Wylie & Lochhead's new Edinburgh store you will find the most comprehensive selection of household furnishings and Electrical equipment displayed against the background of a decoration scheme that in itself provides many practical suggestions for use in the home.

The China Salon on the Second Floor offers a selection of fine bone China, lovely crystal and glass and a variety of colourful earthenware.

Fabrics are on the Third Floor and a wide choice of woven and printed fabrics, damasks, velvets and nets is available.

· · · A HOUSEHOLD NAME

Through no less than Seven Reigns, as a family owned business, we have been manufacturing furniture and bedding and practising cabinet making and joinery. We feel that with this experience we can be of assistance to all who need to furnish or decorate in good taste at a KEEN PRICE

★ FURNITURE is displayed on the FIRST and SECOND FLOORS. CARPETS & LINOLEUM on the THIRD FLOOR and HARDWARE & ELECTRICAL GOODS on the FOURTH FLOOR

WYLIE & LOCHHEAD LTD

25 SHANDWICK PLACE · EDINBURGH

Phone
FOUNTAINBRIDGE 4231

also at Glasgow and Aberdeen (J. & A. Ogilvie)

Phone
FOUNTAINBRIDGE 4231

PART 3: DEPARTMENT STORES

Part 3 has over fifty photographs of Edinburgh's department stores which, hopefully, provide a flavour of how those 'institutions' conducted their business. Many of them are no longer in existence, some have been absorbed into larger concerns, whilst others are still going strong many years after they were founded. By their very nature, department stores were usually opened close to the city centre, mainly in Princes Street, George Street, North Bridge, South Bridge and Tollcross.

This part of the book opens with a group of shops established 'on the Bridges' where it was said, at one time, that a whole family could be kitted out regardless of their budget. Many shops were household names. The opening picture is an artist's impression of the J. & R. Allan empire which, along with Peter Allan's, stretched the whole length of South Bridge from the Tron Kirk to Chambers Street. Although Allan's shops were on South Bridge for many years, the firm actually started in Tolbooth Wynd in Leith. Many residents of Edinburgh will also recall Patrick Thomson's store on North Bridge, but it is unlikely that anyone will remember the previous shop which was on South Bridge, about the position of the present-day Bank Hotel. P.T.'s, established in 1845 by Thomas Thomson at No. 2 Shandwick Place, eventually built a reputation and a customer base far wider than the city of Edinburgh.

THE ARCADE, PRINCES STREET
John Wight, 'Scotland's Premier Tartan Warehouse' is at No. 104 and David A. P. Anderson, Fancy Leather Goods Manufacturer, is at No. 105. Between the two is the entrance to The Arcade where Anderson also occupied units 15 and 16.
Courtesy of Louise Jenkins.

Edinburgh's premier shopping area was, however, Princes Street, with many names which have passed into history: Small's; Forsyth's; Mackay & Chisholm; Woodhouse; Thornton's; Methven & Simpson; Darling's and many more – sufficient to fill a whole book. The stores which have been included are a representative sample rather than an exhaustive list. Fraser's at the West End still flourishes many years after the first department store was opened there by Robert Maul & Son Ltd. in 1893. The shop became Binns in 1934, was taken over by House of Fraser in 1953, and renamed Frasers in 1976. Being on such a prominent corner, the shop has been a favourite Edinburgh meeting place for more than a century. The most famous meeting place for tea was, however, Mackie's at No. 108 Princes Street which had several tearooms with open balconies facing the Castle. Another name which has disappeared from Princes Street is Thornton's which was on the corner with Hanover Street. Although it was best known for waterproof clothing of all types, it also had some innovative lines such as horse-shoe pads and dogcart aprons. Photographs are also included of Woolworth's '3d and 6d store' at the East End, opened in 1926 and closed in 1984. The last few pages in this part consists of a selection of photographs taken over the years of Jenners which has been in Princes Street since 1838.

Other important shops are included,

outwith the area of the Bridges and Princes Street, notably the very extensive branch network of St Cuthbert's Co-operative Association Ltd, which became Scotmid Co-operative Society Ltd. In addition to its numerous food shops, dealt with in Part 1, it had department stores at Bread Street, Nicolson Street, Gorgie Road, George Place and Hamilton Place. Of much more recent origin was Goldberg's in Tollcross. The shop opened in the early 1960s in anticipation of the regeneration of Tollcross, but closed in 1990 – more than a decade before the regeneration arrived! No study of Edinburgh's department stores would be complete without reference to James Gray & Son, Ironmongers, which has been in George Street for more than a century and in existence for more than two centuries.

✦ JENNERS

Jenners, on the corner of Princes Street and South St David's Street, 2005. *Photograph by Ian Goddard.*

J. & R. ALLAN LTD

The illustration comes from J. & R. Allan's advertising material, probably in the 1890s. It shows the extensive premises, Nos 80–86, on the west side of South Bridge. James Spittal, a silk mercer, who later became Lord Provost of Edinburgh, established his business in this section of South Bridge in the early 1800s. He was followed by Alexander & Macnab, silk mercers, at No. 84, and C. & T. Hodge, also silk mercers, at Nos 85 and 86. Around the same time, Meldrum & Allan, drapers, was at No. 35 Tolbooth Wynd in Leith, before purchasing the South Bridge premises in 1876. After the death of Meldrum in 1880, the remaining partner, James Allan, went into partnership with Robert Allan (no relation) to form J. & R. Allan, which became a limited company in 1897. For almost a century, Allan's had a significant presence on South Bridge. In 1970, J. & R. Allan and the sister company, Peter Allan, both of which, by that time, were owned by House of Fraser, merged to form Allan's of the Bridges. Unfortunately, the shops closed in 1976.
Malcolm Cant Collection.

J. & R. Allan Ltd

This artist's impression of the 'grand saloon', built by James Spittal in 1830, has almost as many assistants in attendance as customers, whose comfort and care are obviously paramount. In 1890 an independent review of Edinburgh shops concluded that: 'A visit to this part of the premises will not readily be forgotten and cannot fail to leave behind it pleasing memories of superb fittings and artistic decorations, enhanced by the exhibition of goods of the most attractive description.' There was a combined staff of 210 for the many departments which included dresses, silks, curtains, mantles, furs, gloves, laces, ribbons, haberdashery, trimmings, family mournings, tapestry, floorcoverings, iron bedsteads, napery and millinery. In true Edinburgh fashion, the firm announced that it enjoyed 'the patronage of an exceptionally large, influential and superior clientele.'

J. & R. Allan Advertisement

By the time of this 1930s advertisement, J. & R. Allan had renovated its South Bridge premises (Nos 74–87) and had extended round the corner into Nos 1 and 3 Chambers Street. The grand opening to the extended premises, by invitation only, was on Monday 25 September 1933. The advertisement offers a full bedroom suite for a little over £38.

Malcolm Cant Collection.

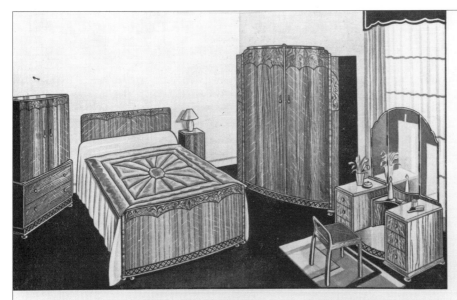

This Handsome Suite in Oak and Ash Price
£27 19 6

Bed to Match
£5 5 0

Dressing Stool
£1 11 6

Bedside Pedestal Table
£3 15 0

Have your home furnished in the modern way by J. & R.'s. Come along and inspect, at leisure and without any obligation, our extensive collection of fine furniture.

J. & R. ALLAN LIMITED SOUTH BRIDGE and CHAMBERS STREET **EDINBURGH**

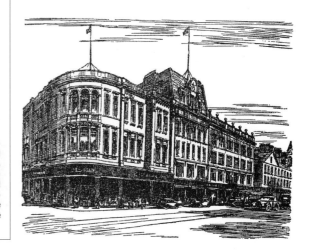

HUGH ROSS & SON

The illustration shows the premises of Hugh Ross & Son, Linen Warehousemen and Outfitters, at Nos 1, 3 & 5 Nicolson Street, with the extensive renovations to the shop planned at the beginning of the twentieth century. The firm could trace its history back to 1851 when Ross & Scott, the linen merchants, occupied a small shop at No. 3. Ross & Scott appear to have been the continuation of a similar type of business, established in 1745, run by Richard Waterston in the High Street. The firm became Hugh Ross & Co. in 1858, and when Hugh Ross's son, John, became a partner around 1874, the name of the firm was changed to Hugh Ross & Son. Some idea of the style of the shop can be inferred from a late nineteenth-century advertisement which claimed that: 'A noteworthy feature [of the shop] is the air of good taste and refinement which prevails throughout the establishment, over which the principals exercise watchful personal supervision'.

Hugh Ross & Son ceased to occupy the Nicolson Street premises around 1909, after which there was a succession of occupiers until John D. Blair & Son moved in around 1913. Blairs, the well-known drapers and outfitters, was one of the many successful department stores 'on the Bridges' until it was forced to close on Saturday 3 August 1968, a victim of 'high costs of overheads and rates'. At the time, a spokesman for Blairs announced that 'the type of store for the future is more of a J. & R. Allan kind'. *Courtesy of Kate Cavaye.*

HUGH ROSS & SON

Right. All floors could also be reached by one of Messrs Waygood's improved direct coupled Passenger Electric Elevators, designed to run at low speed 'to avoid the disagreeable sensation of qualm, which occasionally occurs when a high speed is used'. The safety precautions were said to be vastly in excess of that required by the Board of Trade: the cage was hung by four independent steel wire ropes, each of which was capable of bearing a load ten times greater than the weight of the cage when fully laden. Even if all four ropes broke, the cage was capable of locking itself to its guiding supports.
Courtesy of Kate Cavaye.

HUGH ROSS & SON

Far right. The ground floor main staircase led to an additional three floors, each with 'electric lighting, modern ventilation and the newest system of heating, namely, Dr Clark's Duplex Grates'.
Courtesy of Kate Cavaye.

❧ HUGH ROSS & SON

The immaculately laid out 'blanket and sheeting saloon' was on the second floor. The sales brochure of the day includes: corsets, blankets, sheetings, table linen, towels, counterpanes, down quilts, curtains and all fancy linen goods. *Courtesy of Kate Cavaye.*

❧ JOHN ADAIR & CO.

The impressive corner premises, known as University House, at the corner of South Bridge and Chambers Street, were occupied by John Adair & Co., Merchant Tailors, Hosiers and Hatters. The Adair family had been involved in the tailoring business in Edinburgh for many years. John Adair started the business at No. 227 High Street, *c.* 1850, and was followed by his son, also John, at North Bridge. John Adair & Co. were operating from the South Bridge premises from 1878 and remained there until 1918 when they moved to Leith Street. After Adair moved from South Bridge, the shop was taken over by the Apex Shoe Co. (see page 42), then for a short while by Style & Mantle, and finally by J. & R. Allan.

❧ JOHN ADAIR & CO.

According to Adair's advertising material in the early twentieth century, the 'leading features' of its products were 'artistic finish, reliable materials and moderate charges'. Scotch Tweed suits cost 63 shillings (£3.15p), trousers 15/6d (78p), and ladies' costumes 70 shillings (£3.50p). The advertisement illustrated also gives full details of 'The Highland Costume for Gentlemen and their Sons'.

❧ PATRICK THOMSON LTD

Patrick Thomson's first shop on the Bridges was at Nos. 89–91 South Bridge on the corner with the High Street. The site was later developed by the Bank of Scotland for a branch office and is now the Bank Hotel. *Courtesy of Robin Sherman.*

❧ BON MARCHE LTD

Below left. When Patrick Thomson's was occupying Nos. 89–91 South Bridge, the much grander premises on the east side of North Bridge were occupied by the London firm, Bon Marche, famous for their drapery and fancy goods.
Malcolm Cant Collection.

❧ PATRICK THOMSON LTD

Below right. The picture postcard, from which this photograph is taken, bears the message: 'Isn't this a lovely shop; a band plays all day'. The photograph shows the Cash Drapery Stores at the height of its popularity, shortly after the additional shop units had been acquired. *Malcolm Cant Collection.*

P. T.'s THE SHOPPING CENTRE OF SCOTLAND

PATRICK THOMSON LTD

PATRICK THOMSON LTD EDINBURGH
GENERAL DRAPERY · MILLINERY & COSTUMES · LADIES' OUTFITTING · GENTS' OUTFITTING ✢
BOOTS AND SHOES · FURNITURE · BAZAAR GOODS · HAIR-DRESSING ✢ LUNCHEON & TEAROOMS

✃ PATRICK THOMSON LTD

The very grand North Bridge premises became synonomous with Patrick Thomson's Stores, but the Thomson family name had been in the Edinburgh retail trade for many years prior to their arrival on the Bridges. In 1845 Thomas Thomson set up in business as a silk mercer and linen draper at No. 2 Shandwick Place before moving to No. 135 Princes Street in 1848. By 1890 the firm was Thomson & Allison but the partnership does not seem to have lasted long as Patrick Thomson 'of the late Thomson & Allison' was in business at Nos 89–91 South Bridge by 1900. Patrick Thomson died suddenly, age 46, at his house at No. 18 Hermitage Road on 7 March 1907, after which the business was run by A. F. Gardner until his retirement in 1944. When Mr Gardner retired at age 79 he had been in the drapery business for sixty-five years. Patrick Thomson's became part of the House of Fraser in 1952, changed its name to Arnott's in 1976, and closed in 1981. *Malcolm Cant Collection.*

The Lounge P.T.s

✃ PATRICK THOMSON'S RESTAURANT AND LOUNGE

The restaurant and adjacent lounge were popular features of the North Bridge store from inception. The restaurant was described as 'spacious, comfortable and cheerful' and the lounge 'palatial for ladies and gentlemen – smoking permitted'. In the restaurant, a small orchestra played requests from diners who passed a note of their favourite melodies to the waitresses. In the early 1930s, tea and scones cost one shilling (5p) and High Tea was one shilling and six pence (7½p). By 1937 the restaurant had introduced a special 6-course meal for two shillings and sixpence (12½p). In 1967 the store, in co-operation with the Scottish Milk Marketing Board, introduced their special 'slimming meals'. As an added attraction, for some people at least, two 'Pinta' girls, in distinctive white mini-skirts and hats, were employed to mingle with the diners and hand out recipe leaflets. Also in the late 1960s, a decision was taken to re-introduce music to the restaurant after a lapse of almost twelve years. Andy McRoberts was appointed resident organist and request cards were placed on the tables. Top of the charts, rather predictably for the period, was 'The Sound of Music'. *Left, courtesy of Robin Sherman. Right, courtesy of Pat Scoular.*

❧ THORNTON & CO.

This 1909 photograph shows the premises of
Thornton & Co. (complete with the original open
basement and entrance steps) at No. 78 Princes Street
on the corner with Hanover Street. The business of
patentees, waterproofers and india-rubber manufacturers was established by George Thornton in 1848
and had branches in London, Leeds, Bradford and
Belfast. Thornton's national and international
reputation was greatly enhanced by winning several
medals at the International Fisheries Exhibition in
1883 and the International Forestry Exhibition in
1884. Its main products were belting for machinery,
sheet rubber, delivery and suction hoses and
waterproof clothing of all varieties, especially for the
armed services and the police force. Thornton's
manufactured many of its own products in
Edinburgh and Belfast, securing lucrative patents for
the 'Climax' draught excluder, various styles of horse-
shoe pads and tennis court markers.

❧ THORNTON & CO.

By the time of this 1950s view of Princes Street,
Thornton's premises (the light-coloured building
opposite the Royal Scottish Academy) had been
redesigned to remove access to the basements from
Princes Street and to build out the windows at first-
floor level. *Photograph by Duncan McMillan.*

DO NOT ALLOW YOUR
HOLIDAY TO BE
SPOILED BY
RAIN

You can be independent of
the weather by purchasing
**A THORNTON
WATERPROOF**
Price 12/11
Guaranteed Waterproof

A unique Selection of
Waterproofs, Raincoats and
Oilskins is always in stock

*TARTAN NOVELTIES
AND GIFTS*
are to be found in endless
variety
AT THORNTONS

THORNTON'S
No. 78 IN THE CENTRE OF
PRINCES STREET
Opposite R.S.A. Galleries

J. W. Mackie & Sons Ltd

The firm of J. W. Mackie & Sons Ltd., or Mackie's as it was generally known, was at No. 108 Princes Street for well over a century. It was founded in 1825 by J. W. Mackie in Greenside Street, moved to No. 9 Scotland Street in 1829, to No. 8 Hanover Street in 1835, and finally No. 108 Princes Street in 1840. It is said that No. 108 was previously the home of Lord Woodhouselee, a Senator of the College of Justice. The Princes Street premises were very extensive, four storeys in height, with a 60-foot frontage, and a depth to the Rose Street lanes of 144 feet. The bakeries were at the back and Mr Mackie's own office overlooked the main shop floor so that he could see everything that was going on. In 1865 he brought his two sons, James Wyse Mackie and George Mackie, into the business which became a limited company in 1900. The photograph, entitled 'Ices on the Balcony During Summer', shows the original cast-iron balconies and pillars, described in the advertising material as 'a delightfully cool and pleasant vantage-point whence to survey in summer time the "passing show" of Princes Street'. *Courtesy of Louise Jenkins.*

Mackie's Roof Garden

Far left. The roof garden, with its uninterrupted view of Edinburgh Castle, was a popular venue for many years, offering a wide selection of Edinburgh Shortbread, Scotch Oatcakes, Scotch Bun, gingerbread and Veda bread 'most easily digested'. There was also a large export department in addition to home sales with 'the constant support of a widespread and distinguished clientele representing the aristocracy and the higher social circles generally'. *Malcolm Cant Collection.*

Mackie's of Princes Street

Left. In this photograph taken on Saturday 2 May 1953, Mackie's balconies have been enclosed for protection against the elements but the roof garden and restaurants were still operating under the slogan: 'When you come to Edinburgh ... Come to Mackie's for meals, served in charming rooms ... for perfect views of the Castle, the Gardens, and Princes Street ... and to send home some Mackie's Edinburgh Shortbread.' The advice has obviously been heeded, judging by the queue outside the shop. *Photograph by George Fairley.*

A. GOLDBERG & SONS LTD

Goldberg's store at High Riggs, designed by J. & F. Johnston & Partners in 1960, was a concept 'before its time' intended to be a showpiece in the new road system proposed for Tollcross. When the new traffic plans fell by the wayside, Goldberg's was left in an unenviable position. Its modern construction, over five main floors, allowed for large areas of uninterrupted floor space which was not always available to the more traditional stores on Princes Street and the Bridges. This advantage was exploited to the full, along with other innovative ideas like the roof garden, nursery and menagerie. Unfortunately, within fifteen years of its opening there were serious questions being asked about its viability, especially following completion of the St James Centre in 1970. In the mid-1970s Goldberg applied for, but was refused, permission to convert and let out its two top floors as offices. The management returned to the theme on several occasions, including an intended refurbishment in 1989, but the store closed in 1990. *Courtesy of Pat Scoular.*

A. GOLDBERG & SONS LTD

This once-proud edifice, shorn of its copper sculptures, awaits demolition by Scotdem in 1996. There were serious attempts to save the building, without success. As part of Edinburgh's failed bid to be City of Architecture and Design 1999, the architect David McGill drew up plans to transform the building into an exhibition centre, film and music studios, and a restaurant, but the idea was never taken up. *Photograph by Pat Scoular.*

GOLDBERG'S ADVERTISEMENT

In its hey-day Goldberg's included its own store in 'Places to Visit while in Edinburgh', along with other attractions like Edinburgh Castle and St Giles Cathedral. In the mid-1960s Goldbergs were including several innovative ideas in their advertisements in addition to the traditional offer of good service and a wide variety of stock: 'car park for 60 cars; constantly changing attractions for the children'. *Malcolm Cant Collection.*

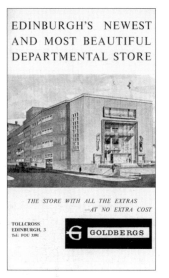

F. W. Woolworth & Co. Ltd

A large crowd has gathered at Woolworth's store at the East End of Princes Street on its opening day on 13 March 1926. The fascia carries the slogans: '3d and 6d stores', and 'Nothing over 6d'. When the store first opened, assistants were paid 14 shillings (70p) for a six-day week and charge-hands (in charge of two assistants) were paid 17 shillings and six pence (88p). *Malcolm Cant Collection.*

F. W. Woolworth & Co. Ltd

This traditional view of Princes Street in 1937 shows, from left to right: the Scott Monument; Jenner's; Forsyth's; the Royal British Hotel; the Palace Cinema; and F. W. Woolworth & Co. Ltd., still advertising itself as the '3d and 6d store'. *Courtesy of Louise Jenkins.*

F. W. Woolworth & Co. Ltd

The topping out ceremony for Woolworth's building at the East End took place on 18 February 1926. Part of Register House can be seen on the left, and the General Post Office on the right. Woolworth's was built on the site of what had been the Crown Hotel, Watt Bros., the drapers, and the Domestic Bazaar Co. An extension was built to the west in 1956 on the site of the former Palace Picture House, and the store closed in 1984. *Malcolm Cant Collection.*

PRINCES STREET LOOKING WEST, EDINBURGH.

221232.J.

❧ ROBERT MAULE & SON LTD

Right. This unusual view of Maule's premises at the
West End of Princes Street was taken in 1906. From
left to right it shows: Shandwick Place; the West End
clock; the extensive five-storey department store of
Maule's on the corner with Hope Street; and, on the
extreme right, a branch of Ferguson's, the confectioners. Robert Maule opened his first business at
Kincardine in 1856 and moved to Nos 74–76 Tolbooth
Wynd, in Leith, in 1872. His big break came in 1893,
however, when he secured the prestigious Princes
Street premises. After Robert Maule died in 1931
control of the business passed to his son, also Robert.
Courtesy of Robin Sherman.

❧ ROBERT MAULE & SON LTD

Below left. The illustration comes from a 1908
advertisement in the form of a postcard, the reverse
side of which shows a young girl clutching her
favourite teddy-bear, beside which are the words:
'Meet me at Maules'. Maules, Binns and Frasers
appear to have been popular meeting places for
several generations. *Malcolm Cant Collection.*

❧ ROBERT MAULE & SON LTD

Below right. Another advertising card shows Maules
West End premises decked out 'On the occasion of
the Royal Visit, July 1927. The premises extend into
Hope Street where the name, Robert Maule & Son,
appears on the face of No. 3 constructed for the Royal
Bank of Scotland which occupied the ground floor.
Courtesy of Robin Sherman.

WEST END, PRINCES ST, EDINBURGH.

BINNS LTD

In 1934, only three years after the death of Robert Maule, the business of Robert Maule & Son Ltd was bought by H. Binns, Son & Co. Ltd. of Sunderland which already had several large branches in England. At the time, the Edinburgh press observed that: 'The acquisition of Maule's by Binns & Co. marks the first entry to Edinburgh by a big English drapery store'. As seen in the photograph, Binns completely revamped the frontage in a near-classical style designed by the architect, John Ross McKay. In 1962 (after the removal of the West End clock to a new position in Leith Walk) Binns installed a very innovative 'replacement' on the corner of their premises, which turned out to be rather controversial. At 7 and 37 minutes past the hour, miniature pipers circled the base of the clock to the tunes *Scotland the Brave* and *Caller Herrin'*. After many complaints from residents and, apparently, civil servants working in St Andrew's House more than a mile away, the volume was toned down to a more acceptable level. *Malcolm Cant Collection.*

HOUSE OF FRASER

Left. Frasers store in its modern setting at the West End, 2005. *Photograph by Ian Goddard.*
Below. Binns Ltd photographed shortly after the company acquired the business of Robert Maule & Son Ltd in 1934. *Malcolm Cant Collection.*

✿ St Cuthbert's Co-operative Association Ltd

The line drawing shows the head office of the Association at No. 92 Fountainbridge in the familiar baronial style of the architect, Hippolyte Blanc, in 1880. A small section of Fountainbridge Free Church can be seen on the right. The Co-operative's first shop was much less grand, opened on 4 November 1859 at No. 50 Fountainbridge on the corner with Ponton Street (see page 10). After several years of mixed fortunes, St Cuthbert's embarked on a programme of expansion with new buildings at Bread Street and Nicolson Street in 1891. Diversification followed with the laundry opened at Chesser in 1912, the Port Hamilton bakery in 1925, the dairy in 1927 and further expansion of the Bread Street store in 1934. Post Second World War development saw huge increases in turnover and an increase in staff numbers to almost 4,000. In 1975 Leith Provident Co-operative was absorbed by St Cuthbert's which became Scottish Midland Co-operative Society Ltd in 1981. At present Scotmid is embarking on a large-scale redevelopment of its head office site in keeping with the changing face of the Fountainbridge area. *From* First Fifty Years of St Cuthbert's Co-operative Association Ltd., 1859-1909.

✿ St Cuthbert's Co-operative Association Ltd, Bread Street

The first Bread Street branch was opened in 1880, followed by this much grander building in 1891 to house various clothing and furniture departments. The building to the right, in less detail, is St Aidan's Church which was acquired by St Cuthbert's in 1934 and demolished in 1937 for a new furnishing department. After demolition of St Aidan's Church the congregation built a new church at Stenhouse. *From* First Fifty Years of St Cuthbert's Co-operative Association Ltd., 1859-1909.

❧ St Cuthbert's
Co-operative Association
Ltd, Nicolson Street
Top left. The photograph shows a
spacious shoe sales area with seats
and foot-stools, and, in the centre,
an X-ray machine for checking to
see if the proposed purchase was
a good fit.

❧ St Cuthbert's Colinton
Mains Grocery
Top right. When the Colinton Mains
grocery branch was opened in the
late 1950s it was one of the
Association's forty-three self-service
stores.

❧ St Cuthbert's Dairy at
Fountainbridge
Bottom left. St Cuthbert's opened its
own dairy at Fountainbridge in 1927
from which it produced 12,000
gallons of pasteurised milk daily for
its shops and home deliveries. Most
of the milk came from its own farms
on the outskirts of Edinburgh

❧ St Cuthbert's,
Leven Street
Bottom right. The interior of the new
superstore built on the site of a
previous store in 1959.
All pictures from One Hundred
Years of Co-operation 1859-1959.

James Gray & Son, Ironmongers

The photograph shows the imposing premises of James Gray & Son, No. 89 George Street, in 2003. The building was designed, *c.* 1902, by the architects Cousin, Ormiston & Taylor, to house the combined firms of James Gray & Son and Smiths & Company.

James Gray established his business as a smith and locksmith in 1818 at Paul's Work at the foot of Leith Wynd, the upper portion of which followed the approximate line of present-day Jeffrey Street. He later moved to the corner of York Place and York Lane where the business was greatly expanded with the assistance of his son, Alexander, who joined the firm in 1836. For a short time in the 1840s James Gray & Sons was in Queen Street but in 1846 it moved to No. 85 George Street, only a few yards from its present address.

Smiths & Company was established in 1770 by Thomas Smith, Tinsmith, in Potterrow. At a very early stage in his career Thomas was engaged in creating improved street lighting and inventing a new system of reflectors for lighthouses, much of the work being done from the Blair Street premises. Around 1875 Smiths moved to No. 89 George Street, and in 1899 it was acquired by James Gray & Son. No. 89 was extensively damaged by fire in 1901 but was completely rebuilt to house the combined firm in 1903. *Courtesy of James Gray & Son*

James Gray & Son, Ironmongers

The amalgamation of James Gray & Son and Smiths & Company brought together two well-established family businesses which had previously specialised in separate, but compatible, lines of stock in their respective George Street premises. The combined, rebuilt premises at No. 89 gave an excellent opportunity to house their wide-ranging stock under one roof. On the left are mantelpieces, over-mantels, pendant lights, urns and dumbwaiters, and on the right, a selection of fenders, pokers, long-handled tongs and coal scuttles.
Courtesy of James Gray & Son.

James Gray & Son, Ironmongers

The frontage of No. 89 George Street, *c.* 1902, shows both names, James Gray & Son, 'with whom is incorporated' Smiths & Company, above which is the Royal Warrant. The left-hand upper window says 'Furnishing Ironmongers and Electrical Engineers' and the right-hand window says 'Purveyor of Lamps and Oils to the King'. The identities of the male members of staff, some senior and some quite young, are, unfortunately, unknown. *Courtesy of James Gray & Son.*

James Gray & Son, Ironmongers

Below left. Four male assistants are on hand in the elegant, pillared, ground floor of No. 89, stacked with individually priced items of ironmongery, heaters and electric light fittings. In addition to their main retail trade, the combined firms held the contract to supply the New Zealand government with a wide variety of stock, and the Northern Lighthouses Commissioners with lighthouse furnishings.
Courtesy of James Gray & Son.

James Gray & Son, Ironmongers

The advertisement, 'I'm a Happy Cook, I use Gray's Ranges', was used by James Gray & Son, *c.* 1903. The photograph was taken by Marshall Wane & Co. of No. 130 Princes Street. *Courtesy of James Gray & Son.*

❧ Jenners, Princes Street, Edinburgh Ltd

The photograph, *c.* 1892, shows the original building on the corner of Princes Street and South St David's Street with the informal annotation 'my bedroom' on the roofline.

The firm, originally known as Kennington & Jenner, opened at No. 47 Princes Street on Tuesday 1 May 1838 'with every prevailing British and Parisian fashion, in silks, shawls, fancy dresses, ribbons, lace, hosiery and every description of linen drapery and haberdashery'. Prior to 1838, Charles Jenner and Charles Kennington were employed by W. R. Spence & Co., silk mercers and linen drapers, of No. 21 Picardy Place but they were dismissed for taking the day off, without permission, to visit the Musselburgh Races. Having no job, but a modicum of ambition, they decided to open their own rival business on Princes Street. The business was not an instant success but gradually they made progress and expanded on Princes Street and South St. David's Street. Charles Kennington retired in 1861 and died two years later leaving the business in the sole charge of Charles Jenner. When Jenner died in 1881 he was succeeded by his partner, James Kennedy, whose descendants ran the business until 2005 when it became a House of Fraser store.

Late in the evening of Saturday 26 November 1892 disaster struck. Almost the entire building was destroyed in a fire which threatened to engulf neighbouring properties. Fortunately no one was killed but the building and the entire Christmas stock was lost, along with the personal effects of about 120 employees. In those days employees who lived out of Edinburgh were accommodated in two dormitories on the upper floors of the building facing South St David's Street – hence the annotation 'my bedroom'. Female members of staff were expected to be in by 10.00 p.m. but the males were given an extra hour to 11.00 p.m. This meant that on the night of the fire the females had to be rescued from the burning building while the males returned to see the whole building ablaze.

❧ Jenner's, Princes Street, Edinburgh Ltd

After the 1892 fire, Jenner's opened a temporary store in what had previously been its warehouse in Rose Street, and what was left of the old building was demolished. A very grand building of six storeys was constructed to designs by the architect, W. Hamilton Beattie, and opened on Wednesday 8 March 1895. The photograph, *c.* 1930, shows the South St David's Street elevation with the later extension to the north in 1903.

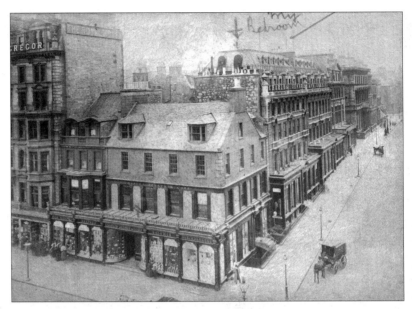

Jenners Grand Hall

Left. This undated photograph by the Edinburgh photographer, J. Campbell Harper, shows the Grand Hall from the Second Gallery level.

Jenners Interior

Below. Coats and capes, in every style and size, in Jenners Coat Department in 1895.

Jenners Interior

Bottom. The Ribbon and Small Accessory Department on the lower ground floor, *c.* 1968.

❧ JENNERS, FASHIONS THROUGH THE AGES
Always at the forefront of fashion: *bottom*, demure
and not easily approached, *c.* 1860; *below*, confident
and stylish, 1957; and, *right*, mannequin parade
promoting dress fabrics from the USA, 1976.
Illustration dated 1860 © Edinburgh City Libraries.
All rights reserved. Photograph dated 1976 courtesy of
A. G. Ingram.

❧ JENNER'S, PRINCES STREET, EDINBURGH LTD
Bottom right. Looking west along Princes Street
with Jenners in the centre of the picture, 2005.
Photograph by Ian Goddard.